SWORD FIGHTING
APPLYING GOD'S WORD TO WIN THE BATTLE FOR OUR MIND

CHRISTINE DILLON

LINKS IN THE CHAIN PRESS

www.storytellerchristine.com

Sword Fighting: Applying God's word to win the battle for our mind

Copyright © 2020 by Christine Dillon

All rights reserved. This book or any portion thereof may not be reproduced or used in any manner whatsoever without the express written permission of the author except for brief quotations in a book review.

Scripture taken from the HOLY BIBLE, NEW INTERNATIONAL VERSION®. NIV®. Copyright © 1973, 1978, 1984, 2011 by International Bible Society. Used by permission of Zondervan. All rights reserved worldwide.

* Many names in this book have been changed.

* Hymn used in the dedication by J. Hart (1723). Public domain.

Cover Design: Lankshear Design.

ISBN: 978-0-6485890-6-8

For my OMF colleagues in Taiwan, Australia, and around the fellowship.

How good is the God we adore!
Our faithful, unchangeable friend:
his love is as great as his pow'r
and knows neither measure nor end.

For Christ is the first and the last;
his Spirit will guide us safe home;
We'll praise him for all that is past
and trust him for all that's to come.

PREFACE

Once upon a time there was an ordinary girl who grew up to be an ordinary woman. She had no outstanding talents but was a good all-rounder.

Her emotions went up and down based on what others thought about her, or even worse, what she thought they thought! Her day could be ruined by an insensitive person saying something like, "Have you put on any weight?" This meant that she constantly felt uncomfortable in public. She had no spare energy to serve others because she was too busy looking at herself.

Her mind was filled with a running commentary. "How could anyone love you?" Or, "You're not special or worth much."

This ordinary girl was crippled by low self-esteem and fear. Her ministry to others was limited because so much of her emotional energy was directed internally.

That very ordinary person was me. It wasn't until I was about twenty-six that I began to learn the lessons in this book. I am still a beginner in many areas and have a long way to go, as anyone who knows me well could tell you, but I wish that someone had explained these issues to me far earlier and spared me much pain.

Perhaps God knew I wasn't ready to absorb these lessons any earlier. I want to share with you some of what I have learned in the hope that you too will be spared unnecessary pain, and will become the men and women that God intends you to be. Living a life that cares more about God's glory and concerns than your own; living a life of selfless service to others instead of trying to make yourself feel better.

If you struggle with issues like fear, doubt, worry, low self-esteem, or discouragement, then this book was written for you.

This book is being produced to accompany my fourth novel and flesh out some of the issues raised in that story.[1]

What this book is not:

- This book is not intended to be a comprehensive discussion of every issue and temptation that someone might face. Rather, it intends to explain the principles and illustrate them by applying them to some of the common problems people encounter. Even if your specific issue is not covered in this book, you should be able to understand the principles and apply them to your particular situation.

- This book is not intended to be a deep theological textbook. Instead, it is intended to be a book that is accessible to the average Christian.

A word of caution

Practical books like this one can be dangerous, as it is all too easy to see them as self-help books, as though, if someone does what is suggested then they'll be a nicer person and have a better life.

It is important from the outset to emphasize that the Bible is not a self-help book. It wasn't written so that you can know how to change yourself and be a more useful human being. It doesn't work if you just dip into it and choose the bits you want for yourself and ignore the rest.

The Bible is neither a talisman to ward off evil, nor a text to be applied like a formula. The Bible is about an awesome God who is concerned with the relationship between Himself and us, His creations. It introduces the God who creates us and wants us to be His children, delighting in Him. Along with everything else that God gives us, is the freedom to choose to love Him as our Father and to serve Him as our King. Tragically, we reject Him as King, placing the crown on our own head, thereby stealing both His job and His glory.

All the problems listed in this book—fear, anger, guilt, depression—come because we've rejected God. For without God, we cut ourselves off from the source of life. We find ourselves dead, the very way we are in fact born—a situation we intrinsically find hard to accept. Unless we accept God's diagnosis of our problem, we will continue treating the Bible as a self-help book, and will grow frustrated when it fails to work.

We are rebellious. Rebels against God and we desperately need a savior. Only God can raise the dead and we are indeed dead, spiritually dead. As we come to understand, in our limited human way, some of what God did for us in sending the Savior, Jesus, and allowing Him to die in our place and take our shame, we will beg God for His forgiveness and mercy.

Once we join God's family, we are promised many gifts but one of them is that we will be "a new creation" (2 Cor. 5:17). We can call on Christ to change us. It is then that the Bible's teaching will be of use to us. God changes His children, so that we become ever more what we should be.

Thus, I urge you right at the beginning, do not deceive yourself that you can be improved without the radical transformation of heart that only Jesus can bring. We cannot change without accepting Jesus as our Savior. If you aren't clear on this point, you may find it helpful to look at some of the following resources before continuing with this book.

- *A Fresh Start* by John Chapman[2]
- www.storyingthescriptures.com has a set of Bible overview historical stories that will take you through from Creation to Jesus' death and resurrection.

- *Christianity Explored* - this is a course, but also includes online resources.[3]
- *Uncovering the Life of Jesus* by Rebecca Manley Pippert[4]

---

1. *Grace in the Desert,* was published in June, 2020. The plan is for there to be six novels eventually, all Australian contemporary Christian fiction. At the back of this book is a list of all the novels and their details.
2. John Chapman, *A Fresh Start* (Sydney: Matthias Media, 1997).
3. Rico Tice and Barry Cooper, *Christianity Explored* (Epsom, Surrey: The Good Book Company/CE, 2016).
   https://www.christianityexplored.org/
4. Rebecca Manley Pippert, *Uncovering the life of Jesus* (Epsom: The Good Book Company, 2015).

PART A: BIBLICAL BASIS

1

THE BATTLE

When someone becomes a Christian, they join a battle. Not a physical battle but a spiritual one. A battle between the habits, desires, and values of our old lifestyle and the new lifestyle that comes because we are now children of God. It is a battle for our hearts and minds. A battle for our desires, emotions, and thoughts.

Ephesians 6 contains the most well-known passage in the Bible about spiritual warfare.

The passage starts,

> Finally, be strong in the Lord and in his mighty power. Put on the full armor of God, so that you can take your stand against the devil's schemes. For our struggle is not against flesh and blood, but against the rulers, against the authorities, against the powers of this dark world and against the spiritual forces of evil in the heavenly realms. Therefore put on the full armor of God, so that when the day of evil comes, you may be able to stand your ground, and after you have done everything, to stand (Eph. 6:10–13).

Let's first consider some of the facts about our situation.

1. We are at war

Paul, the writer of Ephesians, was a realist, so he starts by reminding us that we are in a battle. Not an earthly battle but a spiritual one. Therefore, the enemies, arena, and weapons are all spiritual rather than earthly.

Many Christians seem unaware that they are in a battle. Some may not even believe in the existence of the enemy. Is it any wonder that they are often defeated in their daily lives?

2. We have an enemy

Our main enemy is named in Ephesians 6 as the devil. In Scripture, he has many other names and each name reveals something about his character. Satan (meaning "the adversary"), Lucifer ("morning star") and Beelzebub (perhaps "Lord of the flies," or "Lord of dung") (Matt. 10:25, 12:24, 12:27).[1] General terms are also given such as "prince of this world" (John 14:30), or "ruler of the kingdom of the air" (Eph. 2:2).

There are both numerous references to Satan (as though to prevent us from forgetting him) and brief comments (as though to keep him in his place, far inferior to God). In contrast to Eastern philosophical theories such as yin-yang, God and Satan are not equal and opposite forces.[2] The Bible always presents Satan as a created being, who is vanquished by God.

Ephesians 6 tells us that Satan and his followers (called demons or evil spirits in the rest of the Bible) are rulers and powers of a dark and evil, spiritual world. They are not imaginary but have power, and are a real threat to the unprepared. The rest of the Bible gives us more clues about Satan. As in any battle, the better we know our enemy, the better we can resist him.

The Bible makes clear that God is the only uncreated being. The spiritual powers, known as angels, were created by God to serve him. Like humans, angels seem to have been given free will, and there are hints that Satan used his free will to rebel against God, thus becoming both evil and God's enemy.³ Since then, Satan has been out to destroy God's plans and holds a special hostility for God's people. He is described as the enemy who "prowls around like a roaring lion looking for someone to devour" (1 Pet. 5:8). As the enemy of God, Satan hates seeing us joyful and prayerful and sharing the gospel with others. Instead he tries to bind us (2 Tim. 2:26), making us captive to his will and seeking to blind us to spiritual realities (2 Cor. 4:4).

Satan's Weapons⁴

Satan has various weapons at his disposal and he uses them frequently. Over the millennia, he has stuck with the same weapons because humans fall for them so easily.

a) Lies and Deceit

In John 8:44, Jesus says about Satan,

> ...there is no truth in him. When he lies, he speaks his native language, for he is a liar and the father of lies.

Some of Satan's most successful deceptions mix truth and falsehood because a little truth makes it harder for us to discern the lie.

Satan is described as one who "masquerades as an angel of light" (2 Cor. 11:14). Don't be surprised if his lies sound good and even appear to be the right thing to do.

b) Fear

Satan roars and appears threatening, and we are reduced to a quaking jelly of fear unable to go forward or obey the Lord (1 Pet. 5:8).

c) Doubt

In the Garden of Eden, the serpent said to Eve,

> Did God really say, "You must not eat from any tree in the garden" (Gen. 3:1)?

He wanted Eve to doubt that God was really good and cared about her. Of course, the serpent knew only one tree was forbidden to Adam and Eve but the way he asked the question implied that God is unfair and tyrannical. The seed of doubt was planted and began to do its work. Doubting God's goodness, justice, or power is a favorite Satanic trick. Once doubt sets in, we can feel more justified more in rebelling against God and refusing to do what He says.

3. War is normal for Christians

Returning to Ephesians 6, we see that it is the normal Christian experience to be in a spiritual battle. Indeed, we're thrown into this battle the moment we choose to follow Jesus as our King. Jesus repeatedly warned his disciples of this. If we choose to follow Jesus, then the world will hate us.[5]

> If the world hates you, keep in mind that it hated me first. If you belonged to the world, it would love you as its own...If they persecuted me, they will persecute you also...They will treat you this way because of my name, for they do not know the one who sent me (John 15:18–21).

Satan hates us changing allegiance from darkness to light. He will do anything to bring us back to the darkness and to see God's plans destroyed. We will be actively persecuted, ridiculed, and bypassed because we follow Jesus, the crucified One who was rejected as Lord and Savior.

The difficulty is that a spiritual battle often doesn't seem real. This can be for several reasons. Firstly, we might appear so much like a non-Christian in our values that Satan doesn't waste his time making us aware of the battle. He might just lull us to sleep and hope we drift back into his side of the war. If we aren't actively seeking to read God's Word, relying on God in prayer, living as a follower of Jesus, and sharing our faith with others, Satan has little reason to fear us.

Secondly, we might be unaware of Satan and his work. If we do not know the Bible well enough we can be unaware of spiritual conflicts. We might even falsely attribute things that happen in our lives to being "coincidence."

Paul's words remind us that if we follow Jesus, then we're automatically at war whether we want to be or not and whether we're aware of it or not. However, Paul doesn't leave us with this bad news; he informs us of our responsibility and how we can fight the war.

4. We have been given all we need for this war

There is a constant repetition in Ephesians 6 that the armor we are to wear is the "armor *of God*" (vv. 11, 13) and that it is God's strength and resources that we are using (v. 10). This concept is key to the passage. Unless we do things God's way, we will never see the deep change that is needed. Superficial change will always be exposed as a sham when we come under pressure. It would be like trying to place a band-aid over measles spots. In the short term, a band-aid might cover the existing sore, but it doesn't deal with the underlying infection.

The Bible says from beginning to end that our disease is terminal. Spiritually, we are dead when we are born (Eph. 2:1) despite our ability to cry, move and drink milk.[6] It is only Jesus who can forgive our past, give us new life, and then give us the strength to resist Satan. Before coming to God's new life, we just gave in to Satan because our nature was already twisted in his direction from birth.

In the same way that many people are tempted to think we can save ourselves, we can easily start to rely on ourselves again as we continue on as a Christian. Our ability to resist Satan is totally dependent on the armor that God gives us as a free gift. Like the other free gifts we received when we were adopted as God's children, the armor was graciously and gladly given. We don't need to beg God for His protection and we can't earn it in any way.

Grace is so foreign to our nature that we should not be surprised if we struggle for our whole life to understand it. God's grace comes as a gift that is free to us, but that gift is incredibly costly to God.

5. We are responsible to use the weapons

If we look at the commands noted previously in the Ephesians 6 passage, we get a sense of what our responsibilities are in this war:

> Be *strong* in the Lord and in his mighty power. *Put on* the full armor of God so...you can take your *stand* against the devil's schemes (v. 10-11, emphasis added).

And verses 13–19,

> Therefore *put on* the full armor of God, so that when the day of evil comes you may be able to *stand* your ground, and after you have done everything, to *stand*.
> *Stand firm* then, with the belt of truth *buckled* around your waist, with the breastplate of righteousness in place, and with your feet *fitted* with the readiness that comes from the gospel of peace.
> In addition to all this, *take up* the shield of faith, with which you can extinguish all the flaming arrows of the evil one. *Take* the helmet of salvation and the sword of the Spirit, which is the word of God.
> And *pray* in the Spirit on all occasions with all kinds of prayers and requests. With this in mind, *be alert* and always keep on praying for all the Lord's people.
> Pray also for me, that whenever I speak, words may be given me so that I will fearlessly make known the mystery of the gospel.

Paul repeats the commands as though to drum them into our heads. There seems to be three major kinds of commands: to stand firm, to put on various pieces of armor, and to pray.

a) To stand

At least five times, Paul tells us that we are to stand. There is no mention of advancing and conquering Satan. Defeating Satan is beyond our power; it is Jesus' role. In fact, Satan has already been defeated through Jesus' death and resurrection. The resurrection was the reversal of death and it announced Satan's defeat. The devil's major weapon (death and the fear of it) was smashed when Jesus rose from the dead. Satan is a defeated enemy and so we are told to stand on the victory that Jesus has already won. We can stand with confidence knowing that Satan has no power over us *if* we choose to trust Jesus' past victory on our behalf.

You might ask, "If Satan was defeated at the cross, why does he still seem so powerful and active?" Good question. It is like what happens when you spray a cockroach. When the spray hits the cockroach, you might initially think that the aerosol is a special cockroach energizer! For a few minutes, the cockroach runs around furiously and scares everyone. Suddenly, it lies on its back, wriggles its legs and then is still. Dead! Although for a short time, it might appear even more energetic, experience tells us that it will inevitably die. The battle against Satan is rather similar. The resurrection of Jesus guaranteed that Satan's end is certain. But until that end, Satan seems even more energetic in his desire to destroy God's plans and His creation.

We do not need to fear. If we stand on God's promises found in the Bible, we are secure. Satan cannot harm those who trust Jesus no matter how much Satan tries to convince us that he is as dangerous as a lion. As the Bible tells us, it is Jesus who is the Lion of Judah (Rev. 5:5) and in comparison, Satan is a mere pussycat. Note that the 1 Peter 5:8 passage says he "prowls around like a roaring lion," not that he is a lion. However, if Satan can convince us he is a lion, then he can win a victory over us.

b) To put on the armor

Secondly, we are told to put on various pieces of armor. Although we have been given the armor, some of us put it away in a cupboard and forget about it. Others figuratively leave it in a pile on the ground where it rusts from lack of use. Perhaps some just polish it and admire it, hoarding it as a treasure they never use. But God provided us with the armor both because He knew we would need it, and because He intends us to use it.

So, although we all have the same armor and thus all the

resources we need to stand firm against Satan, we must choose to put on the armor and to stand against Satan. Sadly, many choose (whether actively or passively) not to put on their armor and therefore they are not protected from Satan's lies and doubts. They believe what he says and regularly fall into the sins of worry, doubt, and fear.

We are also urged to put on *all* the armor of God and not just the pieces that appeal to us. All of it is needed if we are to stand firm.

c) To pray

Paul urges us to pray,

> On *all* occasions with *all* kinds of prayers and requests...*always* keep on praying for *all* the Lord's people (v. 18, emphasis added).

This is prayer that is laboring for others as we pray for all Christians, all the time, and with every kind of prayer. It is not the sort of lackadaisical prayer that we mumble before we fall asleep, but fervent prayer offered when we are most alert. It is prayer that knows we are involved in a battle and that prayer is effective. It is prayer that is Biblically-based and not just an airy-fairy "bring world peace." It is the specific, confident prayer of someone who knows their heavenly Father and who sees the spiritual situation clearly.

This prayer is to be "in the Spirit." John Stott comments that our prayer is to be "prompted and guided" by the Holy Spirit.[7] The Holy Spirit convinces us of both the urgent need for prayer and then guides us how to pray in each situation. Prayer in the Spirit will be soaked in Scripture and its principles. It will include both praise to God and a claiming of the promises that are found in Scripture.

Paul also asks the Ephesian Christians to pray that he will have the courage to share the gospel as fearlessly as he should. Were the Ephesians surprised by Paul's prayer request? Did they, like us, place Paul on a pedestal and assume he was never afraid of preaching the gospel? After all, this was the man who had shared the gospel with the Ephesians and had gone to prison for sharing it. Surely he must have conquered fear!

How encouraging it must have been to discover that the great missionary evangelist still struggled with fear and valued their prayers for him. Paul knew that even the best evangelists still struggle with the same fear that they experienced the first time they shared their faith.

Reflection Questions:
1. How often do you remember that you are in a spiritual battle?
2. What dulls people to this reality?
3. Which of the five facts are you most likely to forget? Why?
4. Which of the five facts speaks to you? Why?
5. What would help drive these truths into your life?

You might learn a Bible story and meditate on its truths.[8] For example, Genesis 3:1–15 or Luke 4:1–13.

Prayer Suggestions:
1. Ask God to help you remember the reality of the battle.
2. Praise God for His protection.
3. Claim God's protection.

---

1. https://www.biblestudytools.com/dictionary/beelzebub/
2. Portrayed as interlocking black and white symbols forming a circle. Equal and opposite, darkness and light.
3. Revelation 12 and other passages hint at Satan's past. Also, some passages in the prophetic books (e.g. Isa. 14:12–15 and Ezek. 28) seem to be directed at Babylon and Tyre, but the language used suggests that these countries are examples of a much earlier and more universal pride.
4. For an excellent book on the reality of the spiritual battle and some of the ploys that Satan uses read C. S. Lewis' novel, *The Screwtape Letters*.
    C. S. Lewis, *The Screwtape Letters: Letters from a Senior to a Junior Devil* (Glasgow: William Collins, 2012).
5. The "world" in John's Gospel is anything or anyone who is in opposition to Jesus.
6. Many cultures believe that children are born without sin. However, think back to when a child is young. Does a parent teach their child to be selfish? No, from the earliest of days, good parents teach a child how to do the right thing.

7. John Stott, *The Message of Ephesians,* (Leicester: IVP, 1979), 283.
8. www.storyingtheScriptures.com has many hints about learning stories...and how you can use the stories in your life and ministry.

2

OUR ARMOR FOR PROTECTION

Paul lists six pieces of armor that God has given us for the spiritual battle we are fighting.

Stand firm then, with the **belt of truth** buckled around your waist, with the **breastplate of righteousness** in place, and with your **feet fitted** with the readiness that comes from the gospel of peace. In addition to all this, take up the **shield of faith**, with which you can extinguish all the flaming arrows of the evil one. Take the **helmet of salvation** and the **sword of the Spirit**, which is the word of God (Eph. 6:14-17, bold added).

This extended metaphor is one that Paul's readers, living within the Roman empire, would have been familiar with. There are two major interpretations of Paul's meaning.

Some interpret the pieces of armor in terms of our godliness. Thus, the belt is linked with our integrity, the breastplate is our righteousness, and so on.

However, others focus their interpretation on the gifts that Jesus gives us as a result of his death and resurrection. John Stott argues against an either/or interpretation and for a both/and interpretation.[1]

However, as Paul emphatically says that the armor is God's, the second interpretation seems stronger, although, I too, would lean towards a both/and interpretation.

Five of the pieces of armor can be considered defensive (helmet, breastplate, shoes, belt and shield) and only one offensive (the sword), although it can function in defense as well. This chapter will look at the five defensive pieces and the sword will have a chapter to itself.

1. The belt

A belt may seem a strange thing to label as armor. However, during an era when the soldier wore a heavy leather skirt that protected him from the waist to above his knees, the belt was essential. As well as some extra protection at the soldier's waist, it also prevented the skirt from falling down and the soldier losing the protection that the leather offered. If the leather skirt fell down, then the soldier was likely to trip and end up in a vulnerable position on the ground. In addition, perhaps Paul chose to use truth for the belt because it also held the sword's scabbard in place and thus, is also linked with the "sword of the Spirit, which is the word of God."

Like all the pieces of armor, the belt of truth is God's gift. This "truth" then firstly relates to objective truth that is found in Christ and is linked completely with his word. Satan hates all truth as it is a strong defense against his lies. With the belt buckled in place, we can discern the difference between truth and lies and avoid tripping and falling in our spiritual lives.

With regard to the idea of our truthfulness or integrity, it will always be in response to God's great gifts to us. We value truth highly because of our high regard for Jesus and awareness that He is the one who said, "I am the...truth" (John 14:6).

As followers of Jesus, we are called upon to reflect his character. When we lie or lapse into deceitfulness, we are fighting with Satan's weapons and will be defeated. In contrast, when we are people of integrity who love God's truth, we will be able to defend ourselves against Satan's lies, and he will flee from us.

2. The breastplate

According to John Stott, the Roman breastplate covered both the front and back of the body and protected all the vital organs including the vulnerable heart.[2] Paul uses the term "righteousness" to refer to the justification that comes because of Jesus' death on the cross for us, and as a reminder that we must choose to continue to walk in the way of moral righteousness.

This gift from God is beautifully summarized in 2 Corinthians 5:21,

> God made him who had no sin to be sin for us, so that in him we might become the righteousness of God.

It is hard for us to grasp that our sin can be transferred to Jesus and his righteousness bestowed on us. How can God look at a Christian and not see a sinner but only His beloved child?

The Chinese character for righteousness communicates this well. It is made up of two parts: the lower is the character for *I/me* and the upper character is *lamb*. Jesus is referred to as the "Lamb of God" in several places (John 1:29; 1 Pet. 1:19). Thus, we are made righteous, right with God, when the lamb is over me and God looking down sees Jesus, not me, and so, declares me righteous.

How then are we to put on this piece of armor? We must constantly remind ourselves that we can stand justified and without shame before God because of what Jesus has done for us, not because of any righteousness of our own. If we rely on ourselves, our "righteousness" is a mere embarrassment of "filthy rags" (Isa. 64:6).

Why is this not a once for all action? Because Satan doesn't give up easily. He will constantly attack us.

As Satan accuses us, we can defeat him with God's word from Romans 8:1, 33.

> Therefore, there is now no condemnation for those who are in Christ Jesus...Who will bring any charge against those whom God has chosen? It is God who justifies.

That is confidence indeed. However, it is only confidence and protection for one who is in Christ Jesus.

If we persist in relying on our own goodness, we stand naked before Satan's accusations. For our goodness is a joke. It is so often tainted with selfishness and other wrong motives, as to be useless. It is *only* in Jesus that we have any protection.

Max Turner argues that the idea of righteousness here is holiness and integrity.[3] These effectively defeat Satan because they proclaim our new life in Christ. This righteousness is a response to God's gracious gift of Jesus' righteousness. In other words, we are to live what we already are. Thus, Paul has already said in Ephesians 4:24, "to put on the new self, created to be like God in true righteousness and holiness." It is interesting that he uses the same verb "put on" for the clothing in chapter 4 and the armor of chapter 6. This clear command requires our participation. We are not forcibly dressed but must choose to dress ourselves in holiness in grateful response to all that Jesus has done for us.

God's gift of righteousness and our holiness of life are linked, but it is God's gift which is the most important because without it, our holiness of life would be impossible. Our holiness is only ever a response to God's generous gift.

3. The shoes

Good footwear enabled the soldier's feet to be planted firmly, thus allowing him to wield his sword and use his shield effectively. Apparently there can be two main translations of this verse and they give two slightly different nuances.[4] First, the verse could read, "Let the shoes on your feet be the gospel of peace, to give you a firm footing" (NEB).[5] Thus, it is a knowledge and dependence on the gospel that gives us the necessary steadiness to defend ourselves against Satan's attacks. A deep understanding of the gospel and the peace it brings, both with God and with each other (Eph. 2:14–17), that enables us to stand firm. Once again, this understanding comes through a constant preaching of the gospel to ourselves, and a deep meditation upon it.

The other translation is that we put on the shoes that are our "readiness to announce the Good News of peace" (GNT).[6] This peace is both the peace that we have with God, because our sin problem is dealt with by Jesus' death, and the resultant peace that is then possible between people. This readiness reminds us of Isaiah 52:7, "How beautiful on the mountains are the feet of those who bring good news."

The first translation emphasizes that the shoes give stability to fight. The second suggests the ability to keep on fighting to bring the gospel of peace to people who haven't heard it yet. Satan will hate it that we stand firm on the gospel and continue to share it. We will only be able to persevere if we are convinced of the gospel's truth and keep reminding ourselves of the wonder of it.

U.S. Church leader and author, Jerry Bridges, often mentioned "preaching the gospel to yourself" and he suggested that due to our short memories we needed to do it daily.[7]

4. The shield

The shield in Roman times was made of wood and leather. The leather was soaked in water to help extinguish fiery darts. The word used for shield signifies the full shield which protected the whole body rather than the smaller, round shield.[8]

Satan's fiery darts could include direct demonic attacks, doubts, depression, or any of the temptations we face and that can only be countered by faith in God. This faith is not something we can summon up but is rather a trust directed at God and not ourselves. It is the direction (i.e. what we are trusting in) that matters, not the strength of our faith. As Jesus reminded His disciples, even faith the size of a mustard seed is more than enough if we trust in God (Matt. 17:20; Luke 17:5–6).

5. The helmet

The helmet protects the vulnerable head. This reminds us that we must never forget our salvation. Indeed we must constantly remind ourselves of the truths of the gospel to protect our mind and thoughts. This would include:

- Reminding ourselves that we were rebels against God, separate from Him and unable to save ourselves.
- How much God loves us to send Jesus to die for us.
- Going over and over what Jesus did for us, so that year after year, we understand this more clearly.
- Our status now that we are united with Christ.

In 1 Thessalonians 5:8, Paul refers to the "hope of salvation" as the helmet. So we are to remind ourselves, not only of our salvation achieved by Jesus in the past but that we can be confident that this ensures our full and final salvation when Jesus returns. A firm focus on past salvation, thankfulness for daily salvation, and then confident hope in our full salvation from all sin and pain, will protect our head and thoughts from all kinds of attacks. It will fill us with joyful thankfulness and praise to our gracious, heavenly Father and Savior. Grumbling, doubt and despair will have to flee, to leave us resting in God's peace.

Reflection Questions:

1. Which of these pieces of protective armor means the most to you? Why?

2. How does each piece contribute to the whole armor of God?

3. Say out loud to yourself, "I am the righteousness of God" (2 Cor. 5:21). What is your instinctive reaction to that? Why might that be?

Prayer Suggestions:

1. Praise God for each of these five gifts.

2. Ask God to help you understand how to "put on" these protective pieces in your daily life.

3. Claim God's protection.

---

1. John Stott, *The Message of Ephesians* (Leicester: IVP, 1979), 278.
2. John Stott, *The Message of Ephesians* (Leicester: IVP, 1979), 278.
3. Max Turner, "Ephesians," in *New Bible Commentary* eds. D. A. Carson, , R. T. France, J. A. Motyer, and G. J. Wenham (Leicester: IVP, 1995), 1243.
4. Stott, *The Message of Ephesians*, 280.
5. *New English Bible* (Cambridge: Cambridge University Press; Oxford: Oxford University Press, 1970).
6. *Good News Translation* (New York: American Bible Society, 1992).
7. The author heard Jerry Bridges mention this in an interview at Sydney Missionary and Bible College in either 1996 or 1997.
8. Stott, *The Message of Ephesians,* 281.

3
OUR ARMOR FOR ATTACK

As we saw in the last chapter, five pieces of armor are given for our protection, but only the sword of the Spirit is useful for attack. The "sword of the Spirit which is the word of God" (Eph. 6:17) could be considered to be the key to all the other pieces.

In order to actually put on any of the pieces of armor, we must remind ourselves of the truths of Scripture. Take for example, the helmet of salvation. How do you use this piece of armor to protect the head? Not by reciting a meaningless mantra of "salvation, salvation, salvation" but by remembering all that the Scriptures have to say about salvation. The more we meditate on the great salvation that Jesus has won for us, the better we'll be protected from Satan's attacks.

We remind ourselves of why salvation was needed, reflecting on our rebellion against God and the many ways we work to displace him from the center of our lives. We ponder over the fact that we can never save ourselves through our own efforts and that the only solution is found in God's grace. Then we reflect on how Jesus saved us and his incredible love and mercy towards rebels. The Christian life not only begins with the cross but continues with it until the day we die.

The other pieces of armor—righteousness, faith, shoes of the gospel of peace, truth—are all put on or used by turning to Scripture to remind ourselves of these great gifts that have been lavished on us. These Bible verses will push us to go ever deeper into knowing Jesus and understanding the salvation that comes to us through Jesus' death on the cross.

The sword

The sword is the Spirit's sword and it is clearly identified as God's word. Once again we are reminded that the sword belongs to God. It is His weapon which He graciously gives us to attack Satan.

Not only is the Bible referred to as God's word, but Jesus is called God's Word especially in John 1.

> In the beginning was the Word, and the Word was with God, and the Word was God. He was with God in the beginning. Through him all things were made...

Each phrase adds further clues about this "Word" until verse 14 makes it even clearer that this "Word became flesh and made his dwelling among us." It is at this point that we realize that Word = God = Jesus (God coming as a human to dwell among us and ultimately to save us through His death). The word of God is Jesus himself, though the term is also used for the whole of Scripture. Thus, God's word is found in the Bible and so at the most basic level, we could say that the sword is the Bible.[1] In practice this means that when Satan tells us lies or wants us to doubt or fear, we are to respond by using the truths of the Bible.

Why is the "Spirit" named rather than God or Jesus? It would seem to be linked to the rest of the phrase, "the sword of the Spirit which is the word of God." In John's Gospel in particular, Jesus elaborates on what will happen after He returns to heaven. The disciples will be tempted to feel abandoned, but Jesus says in John 16:6–7,

You are filled with grief because I have said these things [that He is leaving them]. But very truly I tell you, it is for your good that I am going away. Unless I go away, the Advocate will not come to you; but if I go, I will send him to you.

Jesus continues to give them clues about this coming Advocate (who will soon be shown to be the Holy Spirit) and of His role.
Let's consider some of these roles.

1. The Holy Spirit teaches and reminds
In John 14:26 Jesus says,

But the Advocate, the Holy Spirit, whom the Father will send in my name, will teach you all things and will remind you of everything I have said to you.

While Jesus was on earth, He taught His disciples for three years. The Holy Spirit would help them remember what Jesus had said and four of His followers would eventually record what we need to know in the four gospels. Although neither Mark nor Luke were one of the twelve disciples, it seems clear, because of the eyewitness details, that they did extensive interviews with Jesus' followers before writing the books that bear their names.

One of the ways of referring to the Spirit is the "Spirit of Truth" (John 14:17, 15:26, 16:13). He is the Spirit of God and therefore His every word is truth, for God cannot and does not lie.

2. The Holy Spirit convicts of sin
In John 16:8, Jesus says that,

When he [the Holy Spirit] comes, he will prove the world to be in the wrong about sin and righteousness and judgment.

These verses say that the Holy Spirit's role is to prove us in the wrong in three main areas.

a) Sin – The chief rebellion is that we choose not to believe that

Jesus is God and all that He says about Himself. In the context of John's Gospel, perhaps the better word is trust, not merely an intellectual assent but a commitment on the basis of that belief. Failure to trust is the root of all sin and leads to all sinful behavior as we try to run our own lives.

b) Righteousness – In this context, it seems to refer to God's perfect standard. Once Jesus has left the world, the standard of righteousness constantly before the disciples will be gone. Thus, the Holy Spirit's role is to make us look at Jesus and to show us how far we fall short of God's perfect standard.

c) Judgement – The Holy Spirit reminds us that judgement is inevitable and we will all face it. Satan already stands condemned and so being on his side in the war is utter foolishness.

3. The Holy Spirit gives supernatural wisdom when needed

In Luke 12:11–12, Jesus says,

> When you are brought before synagogues, rulers and authorities, do not worry about how you will defend yourselves or what you will say, for the Holy Spirit will teach you at that time what you should say.

Looking at the times in Acts when the disciples were persecuted (e.g. Peter and John in Acts 4; Stephen in Acts 6–7; Paul in Acts 22, 24–26), it is evident that the Holy Spirit helps people remember and share God's word under these abnormally stressful situations.

In 1 Corinthians, Paul talks about the fact that when we share the gospel with others,

> ...we speak, not in words taught us by human wisdom but in words taught by the Spirit (1 Cor. 2:13).

What a relief that the Spirit is our co-worker, giving us the very words of God found in Scripture, just when we need them. Often when we are answering questions from non-Christians or sharing about Jesus, we will be amazed at what we hear ourselves say and we realize it is not our wisdom, but the Holy Spirit reminding us of parts of Scripture that we might not normally recall.

4. The Holy Spirit guarantees that we are God's children

When we trust Jesus for salvation, we are given the Holy Spirit as a gift and a sign that we have God's new life. The Holy Spirit is not just the proof that we are God's children, but is also the means through whom we are raised to this new life. For example, in John 3:3, 5–6 where we're told that,

> No one can see the Kingdom of God unless they are born again....no one can enter the Kingdom of God unless they are born of water and the Spirit. Flesh gives birth to flesh, but the Spirit gives birth to Spirit.

And in Romans 8:9, 14–16,

> If anyone does not have the Spirit of Christ, they do not belong to Christ...those who are led by the Spirit of God are the children of God. The Spirit you received does not make you slaves, so that you live in fear again; rather, the Spirit you received brought about your adoption to sonship...the Spirit himself testifies with our spirit that we are God's children.

Paul is clear, if we are a follower of Jesus then we have the presence of the Holy Spirit within us. This Spirit will remind us over and over again, through the promises contained in God's word, that we are indeed God's children.

5. The Holy Spirit guides us as we follow Jesus and empowers us to live holy lives

Galatians 5 provides a good contrast between what it is like to satisfy the sinful nature and what it is like to walk in the Spirit. We're told to, "Walk by the Spirit, and you will not gratify the desires of the flesh." (v. 16) and those desires are graphically listed in verses 19–21.

Instead of hatred, jealousy, impurity...as we walk in step with the Spirit, we will become like Jesus and these results will be evident in our lives:

> Love, joy, peace, forbearance, kindness, goodness, faithfulness, gentleness and self-control (vv. 22–23).

How do we find out how the Spirit wants us to live? The Spirit will convict us when we drift from God's way and then remind us what it is that God desires. The closer we follow the Spirit's leading, the more we "are being transformed into his [Jesus'] image with ever-increasing glory, which comes from the Lord, who is the Spirit" (2 Cor. 3:18).

6. The Holy Spirit offers comfort and encouragement

Paul suffered greatly for his decision to follow Jesus: shipwrecks, beatings, rejection by his own peers and more. In Romans 8:26, he writes,

> ...the Spirit helps us in our weakness. We do not know what we ought to pray for, but the Spirit himself intercedes for us through wordless groans.

There have been times in my life where the situation is so complicated or the solution so impossible that I didn't know what to pray. It has been such a comfort to admit my inability to say anything coherent and to know that the Spirit Himself is interceding for me.

The Spirit's comfort and encouragement is constant because He always reminds us of God's promises for who we are in Christ and His promises to provide all we need (e.g. 1 Tim. 6:17) and that we will never be forsaken (e.g. Heb. 13:5–6).

Besides the Ephesians passage, there are several other places where the image of a sword is linked with the word of God.

* Revelation 1:16, 2:12, 16

These verses all refer to the vision that John sees of Jesus. Among all the other descriptions is the phrase,

> ...coming out of his [Jesus'] mouth was a sharp, double-edged sword.

The sword coming out of Jesus' mouth seems to be a reference to the word of God being like a sword that discerns motives and deals with falsehood. It suggests judgement occurs against the standard of God's word for comparison. Who would be able to stand in the face of such a standard?

Hebrews 4:12 says,

> For the word of God is alive and active. Sharper than any double-edged sword, it penetrates even to dividing soul and spirit, joints and marrow; it judges the thoughts and attitudes of the heart.

A double-edged sword has cutting ability on every stroke (up and down) and the word of God is able to penetrate even to where we can't see into our hearts. It discerns our thoughts and attitudes and shows them for what they are, often impure and shabby compared to God's standards. This sword is powerful in dealing with our trio of enemies: the world, the flesh, and the devil.

In summary

The Holy Spirit works through the word of God (the Bible) to convict us of sin, urge repentance, comfort us, encourage us and remind us of God's word. Through this, believers will be transformed to be increasingly like Jesus.

I have chosen to focus on the imagery used in the Ephesians 6 passage. Not only is this passage well-known but it uses vivid imagery, which makes it memorable. It clearly states that the enemy is the devil or evil one and his servants. We could easily conclude that this is the only enemy we face. Our enemies could be summarized as the world, the flesh and the devil (Eph. 2:1–2 links these three). The world is a term used to encapsulate that which is in rebellion against God and His ways and which tempts us into that rebellion. It could include religion (relying on self for salvation), or indeed anything which prevents us thinking and facing reality, or anything we use to replace God (e.g. roles, relationships).

The flesh (now often translated, "sinful desires," c.f. Eph. 4:22–24, Col. 3:5) is a somewhat old-fashioned term, but one that is still helpful. It is that part of us that is predisposed to rebellion against God. When Adam and Eve chose to misuse their freedom and listen to the snake in Genesis 3, they set this powerful enemy loose. Today, we all inherit this tendency towards sin.

James 4:1–2 helpfully says,

> What causes fights and quarrels among you? Don't they come from your desires that battle within you? You desire but do not have, so you kill. You covet but you cannot get what you want, so you quarrel and fight.

It will always be tempting for us to see Satan as the sole enemy and in some senses it is true that he is ultimately behind all sin. He is the one who rebelled against God in the beginning. He is the one who tempts us and manipulates the world to offer those temptations. This however skews the tremendous responsibility the Bible places on us.

If we blame Satan for all our wrong thoughts, words and actions, we give him too much credit, and we also downplay our responsibility. Yes, Satan might tempt us through the world and prey on our sinful natures, but ultimately our decision to sin is always our responsibility.

It is only when we are given a new nature by accepting the death and resurrection of Jesus on our behalf, that we are given the power to say "No" to Satan, the world, and our sinful nature. Even so, all too often, we do not use the resources God offers us and we continue to do the wrong thing.

The "sword of the Spirit" wages war against all these enemies. Why did Paul choose to make Satan (and his servants) the enemy in this passage? Perhaps, because the imagery here is so concrete. It is far easier to picture an enemy with personality for this war rather than the vague concepts of the world or the flesh.

I've heard numerous sermons on the armor of God, but the metaphor remained abstract for me. It wasn't until I reached my mid-twenties that I began to apply this metaphor in a practical way. The next chapter will begin to look at these practical aspects.

Reflection Questions:

1. What are the main points that are made about our sword?

2. Which aspects of the Holy Spirit's role are new to you? Which aspects do you sometimes neglect?

3. What parts of this chapter do you need to reflect upon more?

Prayer Suggestions:

1. Turn to Psalm 119 and slowly pray through the verses on the preciousness of God's word. Praise God for his word. This is a long psalm–it might take you quite a few days to pray your way through it.

2. Spend some time meditating on Hebrews 4:12. Turn your meditations into prayer.

3. Ask God to help you understand how to use the sword in your daily life.

---

1. God's "Word" in Scripture refers not only to his "written word - the Bible" and his "incarnate word - Jesus" but also to his "message - the gospel." (c.f. The parable of the sower in Mark 4).

4

USING OUR SWORD IN DAILY LIFE

Despite regularly hearing sermons on the *Armor of God*, there was a disconnect for me. I did not understand how to implement the teaching in my life. After all, how do you put on armor which is spiritual?

Having trained as a physiotherapist, I began to think about sword fighting from a physical point of view and considered things like muscles and fitness.

Imagine if we lived in the Middle Ages, back in the times of knights, and battles on foot and horseback. They did not suddenly go from zero activity to fighting a ten-hour battle. No, they practiced day after day so that when they needed to use their sword, they had the fitness to hold it up all day (swords aren't light) and also the muscle fitness that comes from constant practice of the required movements.

For any kind of exercise, it takes at least six to eight weeks to become fit. Why would sword fighting be any different?

Unskilled sword fighters are just as likely to harm themselves and their friends, as they are to harm the enemy. In the same way, if we want to be skilled at resisting Satan, we can't expect to be skilled after one day. We need to practice daily and build up our spiritual fitness so that we are ready when the battle comes.

Test your sword fighting fitness

During seminars, I will sometimes ask questions like these.

- When the thought "You're useless" comes into your head, what is your immediate response?
- When you're fearful about sharing your faith with a friend, what thoughts come into your mind and what do you do about it?
- How long does it take for you to deal with the lies that enter your head?

When seminar participants are asked questions like these, there is often a long silence and then slowly they come up with some answers. If our responses in battle were that slow, we'd be dead.

The war for the mind is fought in the first seconds, not in a few minutes. If a thought or temptation comes into our mind and we can't immediately combat it with appropriate verses or principles from Scripture, then we are spiritually flabby.

The spiritual battle is a war for the mind. We have to win the war of the mind, or thoughts can too easily become words and actions. As Jesus said in Mark 7:20–23,

> What comes out of a person is what defiles them. For it is from within, out of a person's heart, that evil thoughts come—sexual immorality, theft, murder, adultery, greed, malice, deceit, lewdness, envy, slander, arrogance and folly. All these evils come from inside and defile a person.

When people who have had an affair are questioned, there is often a similarity in the stories. Many report that the affair was the result of many smaller steps; the mind is allowed to dwell where it shouldn't and over time, those thoughts are fed until eventually they grow into actions.

Our goal must be to win the war of the mind, so that the outflow of our wrong thoughts never turns into behaviors. Paul also uses the imagery of warfare in 2 Corinthians 10:3–5 (emphasis added),

> For though we live in the world, we do not wage war as the world does. The weapons we fight with are not the weapons of the world. On the contrary, they have divine power to demolish strongholds. We demolish arguments and every pretension that sets itself up against the knowledge of God, and we *take captive every thought* to make it obedient to Christ. For though we live in the world, we do not wage war as the world does.

It is the action of "taking every thought captive" that is the core of spiritual sword fighting.

Taking every thought captive and demolishing arguments and pretensions aren't for the lazy or weak. It is going to take a great deal of effort and skill. We have to practice. We have to learn how to identify the false thoughts, arguments and pretensions. We need to know the standard of truth (the Bible) in detail and be able to recall its truths quickly in order to be able to recognize lies. Then, we will have to rigorously and effectively apply the truths of Scripture, so that we can take thoughts captive, and immobilize them, so that they cannot wreak havoc within our lives. We do not want a situation like the Great Fire of London in the 16th century, where the fire started in one shop but soon engulfed row after row of wooden houses. If the fire of untrue thoughts in our lives is not immediately controlled, its influence spreads and multiplies.

Jesus as our model

The clearest Biblical example of how sword fighting is done is found in Luke 4. Jesus is about to start His public ministry, but first the Spirit leads Him to the desert where He was tempted for forty days by the devil. During those forty days, Jesus ate nothing. Satan waits until Jesus is at His weakest point before he comes to tempt Him.

Satan throws all his weapons at Jesus including doubt, lies and deceit. Three times Jesus answers Satan immediately with Scripture. Each answer gets below the surface of the temptation and exposes the hidden barb that is waiting to trap Jesus.

For example, in the first temptation Satan suggests that Jesus use His power to turn stones into bread. Jesus recognizes that He is not just being tempted to create food to deal with His hunger. Satan is actually asking Jesus to stop trusting God for provision and to rely on Himself, hence the answer from Deuteronomy 8:3,

> Man does not live on bread alone but on every word that comes from the mouth of the Lord.

This reference is to God's provision of manna in the wilderness. God gave the Israelites specific instructions regarding the collection of the manna. If they were greedy and collected too much, then the excess would rot. However, if they collected double before the day of Sabbath rest, God would miraculously preserve it so that it didn't rot (Exod. 16). The Israelites were to learn to trust God despite the fact that it defied ordinary logic. Jesus uses this text to combat Satan and makes it clear that He too will trust God's ways and not use His powers to provide for Himself.

Satan goes on to promise Jesus that if He just bows to him, then Satan will give Him authority over the kingdoms of the earth. Jesus could have answered, "No way, the kingdoms belong to God," but instead, Jesus quotes Deuteronomy 6:13, about only worshipping God.

In the final temptation, Satan suggests that Jesus jump from the top of the temple and that He will not be hurt because God will send angels to protect Him. In this temptation, Satan masquerades as an angel of light because he backs up his reasoning by quoting Psalm 91:11–12,

> For he [God] will command his angels concerning you to guard you in all your ways; they will lift you up in their hands, so that you will not strike your foot against a stone.

Satan's quote is correct, but the deceit comes because he takes it out of context. He makes it sound as if God promises that He will look after us in any circumstance. However, when you read it in context, you realize that this promise is conditional. Verses 9–10, just prior to Satan's quote are, "If you say, 'The Lord is my refuge,' and you make the Most High your dwelling, no harm will overtake you, no disaster will come near your tent."

The Psalm says that God will only protect those who trust Him, but Satan is saying, "Trust me and not God." There is no guarantee of God's protection for those who trust in something or someone other than Him.

Jesus is God himself and thus could have used any method to answer Satan, for His words have an authority that ours never will. Yet the fact that He chooses to use Scripture, gives us the ultimate model of how we are to stand against temptation.

Becoming spiritually fit

We are to take every thought captive by responding with Scripture to each wrong thought that comes into our head. But how then can we build up our spiritual fitness so that we can do this in the millisecond that we need to?

I have found that the best way is to start somewhat mechanically. If you have ever seen a behind-the-scenes documentary on a film that contains sword fighting, you will be familiar with the process. Those wonderful sword fights in a movie are choreographed as carefully as a dance. Each individual stroke is learned until it is fast and fluid. It is then combined with another stroke until the whole sequence is as familiar as breathing. The actors comment about how much hard work it is and how many days it takes to get fit and skilled enough to make the sword work look beautiful. It is not only beautiful but would be deadly if they were using a real sword in a real fight.

I am including the mechanical steps that I have used. These are not listed in the Bible, so please beware of making them a formula to follow. These steps are not meant to be a substitute for knowing Jesus better, but to help us soak ourselves in His words. They are an attempt to turn an abstract concept into a practical one.

1. Identify the issue

What is your main issue? Is it anger, fear, worry or something else?

Try to dig below the surface. Why do I worry so easily? What does it say about what I believe about God?

2. Identify Bible verses or stories that tackle the issue

Think about verses and Biblical principles that apply to your particular issue and write them down. If you need help, consider asking a friend, or a pastor, or consider searching the internet.

3. Review the Scriptures daily or twice daily

Morning and evening, read through or memorize the verses and think about them. Morning and evening are best because then we are meditating on God's word first thing each day and last thing each night.

Turn each of the meditations and lessons you learn into prayers of thanks and praise to God. Choosing to thank God for His truths is our first step of faith and helps us to cement that truth into our own lives.

J. I. Packer wrote, "I'll give you the rule for turning knowledge about God into knowledge of God. It's simple but it's very demanding. I take every new truth I learn about God and I turn it into meditation before God and then translate it into prayer and praise to God."[1]

Keep doing this for as long as it takes for you to automatically have the verses springing to mind when Satan sends his bad thoughts and temptations your way. I have usually suggested something from six to eight weeks because that is how long it takes us to get physically fit. With constant repetition, God's word seems to move from our head (i.e. being mere theory) to our hearts (i.e. becoming something we really believe).

When an untrue or ungodly thought enters our minds, the aim is to get to the stage of automatically responding with an appropriate Scripture.

Reflection Questions:
1. What issues do you specifically struggle with? Are there issues where you constantly give in to temptation?
2. What solutions have you tried? What have been the limitations of those methods? Why might that be?
3. How spiritually fit are you in the area of taking every thought captive?
4. Work though one issue using the first two steps: firstly identify the issue and then apply Bible verses or stories.
5. Do you think your issue is a sin? Why or why not?

Prayer Suggestions:
1. Repent of the times when you have given in to temptation remembering that God has paid the price for your sin, but also promises to forgive. Reflect on Psalm 103:8–12.
2. Ask God to remind you of verses or stories that speak directly to your issue.
3. Ask God for His help to become more like Jesus and thank Him that this is possible.

---

1. J. I. Packer, *Knowing God* (Leicester: IVP, 1993), 20.

PART B: SPECIFIC ISSUES

The second half of this book deals specifically with various problems that the average Christian faces. Each chapter will contain stories of people who have struggled with a particular issue and list some verses and scriptural principles to help to start thinking about it. Hopefully, you will think of other verses and principles that best suit your particular situation. This booklet will not attempt to look at all the possible issues. Rather, I have chosen some common ones. It is better to use this part of the book as a reference, rather than just reading it straight through, as there will be a degree of overlap on various issues.

5
ANGER

Originally this chapter was much later in the book, but a comment from a pastor led me to change the order. He said that of all the booklets that the church has available, the one on anger is borrowed most often.

As Robert Jones writes,

> Anger is a universal problem, prevalent in every culture, experienced by every generation. No one is isolated from its presence or immune from its poison. It permeates each person and spoils our most intimate relationships. Anger is a given part of our fallen fabric...Sadly this is true even in our Christian homes and churches.[1]

All too often anger bubbles up and we are not even aware what is causing it. Some readers might think, if anger is wrong, why are there so many references in the Bible to God being angry? His anger often burned against the people of Israel (Exod. 32:9ff.; Num. 11:1–3, 10; Num. 12). Jesus also became angry, as in the case of the clearing of the temple (Luke 19:45–48). When read in context, we realize that anger is not necessarily sinful. There are cases when anger can be righteous. How then do we discern whether or not our anger is righteous?

Discerning if anger is righteous or not

It is hard not to be angry when evil seems to flourish and the good suffer.

Righteous anger is concerned with God's glory. For example, during the incident of the Golden Calf in Exodus 32, God is angry (as is Moses) because not only are the people worshipping another god, but they are also declaring that the god who rescued them out of Egypt can be represented by an inanimate object. Such an insult to God.

God is often angered by idolatry (Deut. 32:16 is one example of many), because it not only insults Him but is so senseless. The Israelites were exiled because of their repeated rejection of God despite every proof of His existence and goodness. As they rejected God, their society degenerated into practicing evil and injustice.

2 Kings 17:16–17 describes this,

> They forsook all the commands of the Lord their God and made for themselves...idols...they bowed down to all the starry hosts...they sacrificed their sons and daughters in the fire. They practiced divination and sought omens and sold themselves to do evil in the eyes of the Lord, arousing his anger.

God's anger at evil and injustice should be a comfort to us. He cares greatly about the evils and injustices in the world and won't sit idly by. We don't need to take revenge and are warned not to in Romans 12:19ff. because God will bring justice with His own perfect timing. If we try to take things into our own hands, we will almost always end up doing evil ourselves.

God is also angry when people stubbornly refuse to trust that He has their good in mind. At the burning bush, God eventually became angry because Moses kept giving excuses for not being the leader that God was asking him to be. Instead of trusting God, Moses was totally self-focused (Exod. 3, 4 and especially 4:14).

God's anger is designed to lead us to repentance.

Our motivations

We would all like to think that the majority of our anger is righteous, but even if we start with anger for the right reasons, our motivations often become twisted. So much of our anger is the anger of frustration and occurs when we are not getting our own way.

Moses was guilty of this. In his early years of ministry, he was concerned about God's reputation, but later in life, he indulged in unrighteous anger springing from frustration. God asks him to speak to a rock so that water will gush out and quench the Israelites' thirst (Num. 20). Moses' frustration makes him forget he should be focused on God's reputation. Instead of speaking to the rock, he gets angry and turns it into a theatrical performance by striking the rock. God sees into Moses' heart and says, "Because you did not trust in me enough to honor me as holy in the sight of the Israelites, you will not bring this community into the land I give them" (Num. 20:12).

When anger boils over or knots our stomach, it is worth stepping back and examining why we are angry. All too often, our motivations are not pretty.

Sadly, many children see anger modelled as the primary way to respond to frustration. When no other model of solving problems is presented, they will commonly respond as their parents have done.

Is anger increasing in our society?

The Internet seems to have given many people a soap box to rant about the things that happen to them and sadly, it is easy to gather evidence that your case isn't the only one. I have been saddened to see a growing sense of entitlement in certain circles that perpetuates the cycle of anger.

It is possible to start with righteous anger at injustice, but quickly slip over into generalizing this anger onto other issues or other people who have not perpetrated the original injustice.

Many years ago, I received a letter from an elderly friend with whom I had always had the best of relationships. The letter seemed to be from a stranger. It blasted me for ungratefulness and other accusations that were completely untrue. I was shattered. This letter could so easily have been the end of our long friendship, but thankfully, I had begun to learn about sword fighting.

My new sword fighting skills enabled me to work through the hurt. I soon realized that my friend had obviously not found the thank-you card I had left her. Believing I'd not said thank you for her hospitality triggered all her resentment and frustrations at the modern generation. Instead of keeping to one topic, she allowed herself to attack all those that she saw as ungrateful. I received years of her frustration in one angry torrent.

Many of us have similar sorts of triggers. For me, it is the line "all religions are the same." I have heard this hundreds of times when I share the Good News with people and it drives me crazy because not only is it false, it is also an insult to Jesus and the work He did on the cross. I have to be careful to respond to the person who said it as though they are the first person who has said this to me, rather than the hundredth person. I have to take a deep breath and be gracious. There is no point in becoming angry with someone who is blind or "dead in their sin" (Eph. 2:1). Yelling at a "corpse" will not raise them from the dead. If you yell at your non-Christian friend you'll likely lose any further opportunities to talk about Jesus.

With my elderly friend, it was clear to me that I had a choice. I could either break off our friendship (the easier option) or work through things and respond with graciousness. I am eternally grateful that I chose the latter and did not respond to her on the basis of the way she treated me.

Sadly, much of the anger in our relationships comes because we aren't getting our own way. We can use anger to voice our frustrations, or worse yet, to bludgeon others into doing our will. As Jesus reminds us in Mark 7:14–21, our angry words are a result of an angry heart. We need to look at the heart reasons for our anger.[2] The old cure of counting to ten slowly before we speak might temporarily help us, but it will never deal with our heart. Only God can do that through His word. Sadly, those who are habitually angry are often allowed to continue in their selfish ways because people are afraid to confront them in case they rouse their anger. So in effect, we support and encourage their habit.

The results of anger

Prison, divorce and domestic violence statistics bear out the high cost of anger.

Apart from the obvious affects on our own health, of raised blood-pressure, heart attack, stroke and the many other possible results of stress, our anger can also mean that people reject Jesus because of our behavior.

A Taiwanese friend of mine only knew one Christian before she knew me. One day, as I was sitting next to her, she received a phone call from her Christian friend. I was appalled to hear the Christian's anger reverberating along the line. Eventually the non-Christian lady (who had responded incredibly well throughout the call) just put the phone down. She saw the look on my face and said, "She's been like that for the twenty years I've known her. She says she's a Christian, but I don't see any evidence of it."

Her Christian friend was a major stumbling block in this woman's journey towards knowing Jesus. Praise God, I have recently heard that God has transformed this angry lady. Someday, I hope to hear the story about how it happened. Is our anger bringing God dishonor so that non-Christians reject Jesus because of us?

How much of the crime in the news is a result of anger? Murder, rape, beatings, war and other injustices. I used to live in a small town and one Saturday morning during the busiest market time of the week, a market seller grabbed a knife and attacked another market seller. Not surprisingly, it turned out that there had been a twenty-year war of words between the two. One man had never forgiven the other seller and had allowed his anger to turn to resentment and it poisoned their whole relationship. Eventually it led to the ultimate expression of anger—death from multiple stab wounds and two families destroyed.

It is easy to dismiss this example and pretend that anger is only in the hearts of those outside the church, but sadly it also wreaks havoc within the church.

If we were to take a long look at our relationships at work, church, and home, we would be appalled at the high cost of anger.

Two friends of mine had been married for thirty years. They worked hard at improving their marriage but they had a problem. Every time they built up their marriage and saw real progress, they tore everything down by exploding in anger. Within a few seconds, they would be hurting and back where they started. They realized that they had to deal with their anger problem and also investigate its root causes, as it was harming their marriage and causing them both to feel like failures.

Using our sword

Thankfully, we are not left to battle on our own. The Bible contains much wisdom that can help tackle this devastating problem.

I'll start with a verse that has been a particular help to me in this area, especially when I've been tempted to be angry with government officials or in frustrating committee meetings.

* Proverbs 15:1

A gentle answer turns away wrath, but a harsh word stirs up anger.

It reminds us that when we get angry, it is like adding fuel to a fire. The whole situation quickly becomes explosive. However, when we choose to answer gently (the tone of voice is often more important than any words), it is like dousing the fire with water. The whole situation begins to simmer down.

* Two verses that contain warnings and advice. Proverbs 10:19,

> When words are many, sin is not absent, but he who holds his tongue is wise.³

And James 1:19, 20, 26,

> Everyone should be quick to listen, slow to speak and slow to become angry, because human anger does not produce the righteousness that God desires...Those who consider themselves religious and yet do not keep a tight rein on their tongues deceive themselves, and their religion is worthless.

The more words we say, the more likely we are to say something that we will regret. Learning to slow down, listen and think can stop us from misunderstanding others and so prevent many of the situations where we might otherwise have rushed in and exploded in anger.

* 1 Peter 2:23

> When they hurled their insults at him [Jesus], he did not retaliate; when he suffered, he made no threats. Instead, he entrusted himself to him who judges justly.

Jesus did not respond in anger even when He was falsely accused. He, who never sinned or had wrong motives, was accused of deception and other crimes by people who would use any means to have Him crucified (Luke 23). Their plots succeeded and Jesus was nailed to the cross the following day.

An Australian friend of mine,⁴ gave this testimony in a sermon on anger.

I like to think of myself as a pretty relaxed driver. I hardly ever use my horn, I don't make a practice of yelling at other drivers. But I remember one time last year, sitting in the overtaking lane. I was going at the speed limit, slowly overtaking the cars on the inside lane. Suddenly a car came right up behind me and sat right on my tail. That really annoyed me. I didn't want to go any faster, I'd be breaking the speed limit, but I did not want to pull over and let him pass either, because there were cars there that I was passing. I accelerated a little so it was safe for me to change lanes. I let him pass, then I came right back out again and sat on his bumper bar (fender) to see how he liked it. At that moment I was full of anger. I was behaving foolishly. I was behaving sinfully.

As I thought about it later, I realized that although he shouldn't have sat on my bumper, it's not my job to punish him for doing the wrong thing. If he drives foolishly, he may get booked by the police and if he avoids them, God will eventually judge him, just as He judges us all.

Very often when we are angry, we become judgemental and want to punish.

When you have been wronged, there are times when it is right to gently and lovingly go to that person and talk about it. Jesus says if your brother sins against you go to him, and show him his fault between the two of you (Matt. 18:15). Yet most of the time, our anger wrongly assumes that we are in a position to judge and punish others, when only God is in that position.

Here are some other verses and stories you could meditate upon.
  * Reflecting on stories about the consequences of anger can be helpful. Cain's anger (Gen. 4) led to him killing his younger brother. Saul's anger and jealousy towards David nearly led him to murder (1 Sam. 19) and then erupted at his son Jonathan. Saul hurled a spear at

Jonathan and could so easily have killed his own son (1 Sam. 20:30–33).

*Ephesians 4:26–27

> "In your anger do not sin": Do not let the sun go down while you are still angry, and do not give the devil a foothold.

This verse was a strong principle in our family. I remember many nights as a teenager being unable to sleep until I went and said sorry to various family members. I did not want my resentment and bitterness to grow and fester.[5]

God wants us to keep short accounts and deal with issues immediately so that Satan doesn't gain a foothold into our lives to spread his evil influence even further. Like any enemy, he seeks to establish a beachhead in our lives so that he can launch more attacks from within our thoughts.

I am grateful that God (through my parents) established this principle in my life. What a freedom it would be if we had no bitterness in our lives.

Ephesians 4 does not tell us to merely take off sin but reminds us that we also need to replace our former behaviors with new ones. We must put on new clothes in the place of the old.

Verse 32 tells us how we are to respond instead of being angry.

> Be kind and compassionate to one another, forgiving each other, just as in Christ, God forgave you.

Rather than simply not being angry or bitter, we are to forgive and respond with kindness and compassion.

Such a standard sounds impossible, but the more we use our sword and meditate on what Jesus did, the more possible it will become. It is at the cross of Christ that the victory was achieved so that the power is available for us to learn to love and forgive. The more we reflect on what Jesus did for us, the more we will be moved to thankfulness and a desire to behave in the same way to others. Long meditation (I like to call it "chewing the cud") on the cross and resurrection will lead to major changes in our lives.

And what about my two friends whose marriage was being damaged through anger? Memorizing Scripture and reflecting on it has improved their marriage so that it has become a blessing to them both. They are a testimony of the efficacy of using the "sword of the Spirit which is the word of God."

Reflection Questions:

1. Look up 1 Samuel 8 and 11 as well as 1 Kings 21. Is the anger in these chapters righteous or not? Why or why not?

2. Think about your anger in specific situations. Why are you getting angry?

3. What have been the results of anger in your life?

4. Now list some verses or stories that you will use to sword fight. Decide how you will use them and make yourself accountable to someone to do so. Ask them to check up to see how you are going.

5. Choose a recent example of your anger and think through how you could have responded differently. What part could your memorized Scriptures have played in that?

Prayer Suggestions:

1. Repent of any behaviors that are not pleasing to God.
2. Ask God to help you respond more patiently.
3. Ask God to provide an accountability partner.

---

1. Robert D. Jones, *Uprooting Anger: Biblical Help for a Common Problem* (Phillipsburg: P&R Publishing, 2005), 3.
2. Anger is a complex emotion and can be the outward symptom of fear, anxiety, or shame. It might be important for a person to see a counselor who will ask ques-

tions that probe for the causes of their anger. This will allow the right kinds of Scriptures to be chosen.
3. This is the 1984 version of the *New International Version*.
4. Used with permission.
5. Please note, there are times when a situation has escalated late at night or you're too tired to deal with it, and in that case it would be wise to wait until both parties have cooled down. The principle remains though, that you should deal with issues as soon as possible to prevent lingering problems.

6
WORRY

Is there anyone who is free from worry? We start young and keep worrying until we die. Worry feels so natural.

We worry about *money*. Do we have enough? What if the banks or stock markets or job markets collapse? Even if we have money, is it safe once we've got it?

We worry about *relationships*. Will they like me? Will they keep on loving me? Is my marriage secure?

We worry about the *future*. And if that isn't enough, we spend our time worrying about *what ifs* even though many of these will never happen.

- What if I marry this person, and then they get sick and leave me a widow/widower?
- What if I can't have children, or my child dies, or turns out to be a drug addict, or a killer?
- What if I get cancer, or another debilitating health problem?

The worrier can say in their head, "If I don't do this, then everything will fail." They endlessly rehearse different solutions. Too many nights, I have found myself lying in bed thinking about five possible solutions to a problem and weighing up the pros and cons. It would be much better to turn the matter over to God in prayer and go to sleep. Even when I have prayed about it and think I am trusting God, the problem is being turned over and over in my mind. We think we're placing our problem in God's hand and then we snatch it back again, as though God's hand isn't strong enough.

Worry is saying to God, "I don't trust you to solve this problem," or at the very least saying, "You need my help!" Put like that, we can see the presumptive and ridiculous nature of worry.

This is what Abraham and Sarah did in Genesis 16. God had promised Abraham that he would become a great nation which meant God was promising that they would have a son. But one year passed and then another. After ten years, with the two of them now eighty-five and seventy-five respectively, they had given up. Most of us wouldn't blame them.

So Sarah said to her husband, "The Lord has kept me from having children," and then she came up with her solution.

> Go, sleep with my slave; perhaps I can build a family through her (v. 2).

How often have we done the same? God hasn't answered our prayer and so we want to help Him out. The problem was that their solution wasn't what God had promised. Their worrying and anxiety led them to make a real mess of their family and added more stresses whose impacts even reach down to modern times. The child of Hagar became the father of the Arab peoples and the son of Sarah became the ancestor of the Jewish people. One little decision to go their own way and it has led to 4000 years of conflict.

Worry is a sin because it is a failure to keep trusting God. Abraham should have said to Sarah, "Thank you for being concerned about the problem but let's not rush ahead. Let's go back to God and ask Him. Let's keep trusting."

Let's go through the stages of dealing with the issue of worry:

1. Identify the problem

Once we label worry correctly as a sin, we are on the way to a solution that starts with sincere repentance for doubting God's power and care for us.

2. Identify verses to counter this issue with Biblical truth

Sometimes we might need to start our sword fighting by reminding ourselves of the dangers of anxiety and worry.

* Proverbs 12:25

Anxiety weighs down the heart.

There is a heavy cost for persisting in worrying. Older versions of the Bible use the more descriptive word "burden." Worry is like carrying a huge sack of potatoes around with us. We end up staring at the ground and groaning, without hope or joy.

* Proverbs 28:26

Those who trust in themselves are fools, but those who walk in wisdom are kept safe.

Yet another warning.

It is worth asking why he who trusts himself is a fool. One reason is simply that we are so weak and lacking in wisdom, as we seldom understand the whole situation. Therefore, trusting our own limited judgement is foolish. We'll often make the wrong decision. In addition, we seldom have the strength to carry out our plan anyway. Rather, we are to recognize that our worry is a refusal to trust God and to keep reminding ourselves of His trustworthiness.

* Ecclesiastes 2:22–23,

What do people get for all the toil and anxious striving with which they labor under the sun? All their days their work is grief and pain; even at night their minds do not rest.

The "teacher" mentioned in Ecclesiastes was obviously familiar with worry. If the teacher was Solomon, then he had the responsibilities of a kingdom and a huge family. Worriers make even their nights miserable as they are unable to sleep.

* Hebrews 11:6

Without faith it is impossible to please God.

The essence of pleasing God is taking Him at His word and trusting Him with our entire lives. If we claim to be a follower of Jesus, then we must trust Him or our actions negate our words. First, we must trust Him for our salvation (since we can't save ourselves), then we must trust Him for all our daily needs—physical, emotional and spiritual.

We then need to remind ourselves of God's power and His love and care. Both need to come together because if He is merely powerful, it does not mean He would take any notice of such insignificant things as human beings. I find it helpful to remind myself of Biblical stories like the wilderness wanderings of Israel where God not only provided food for forty years but even looked after the small details which we would have forgotten, like making sure people's clothes didn't wear out and preventing their legs from swelling (Deut. 8:4).

* 1 Peter 5:7

Cast all your anxiety on him because he cares for you.

I like the imagery of these verses with the thought of dumping my big burden of care that is weighing me down, into Jesus' more than capable hands. Just meditating on this verse gives me a sense of relief, like a deep sigh.

* Psalm 32:10,

The Lord's unfailing love surrounds the one who trusts in him.

There are numerous promises that God will love and protect the one who trusts in Him. Conversely, these promises contain a warning that God won't necessarily protect the one who refuses to trust in Him. To trust God or to put one's faith in Him is a choice with consequences.

Jesus knew that humans have a huge tendency to worry, for He devoted a good percentage of His Sermon on the Mount to the topic. Each one of these verses contain principles that could be meditated on slowly.

* Matthew 6:25–26,

Therefore I tell you, do not worry about your life, what you will eat or drink; or about your body, what you will wear. Is not life more than food, and the body more than clothes? Look at the birds of the air; they do not sow or reap or store away in barns, and yet your heavenly Father feeds them. Are you not much more valuable than they?

How much time we waste worrying, and how willing God is to supply our needs. Like the Israelites in the desert, He is just waiting for us to trust Him. Every day, God cares for the whole of creation and Jesus tells us we are more precious that they are. These verses are both a rebuke for our lack of faith and a reminder that we have a loving heavenly Father who is more than able to look after us.

Matthew 6 continues in verses 27–30,

Can any one of you by worrying add a single hour to your life? And why do you worry about clothes? See how the flowers of the field grow. They do not labor or spin. Yet I tell you that not even Solomon in all his splendor was dressed like one of these. If that is how God clothes the grass of the field, which is here today and tomorrow is thrown into the fire, will he not much more clothe you—you of little faith?

Once again Jesus goes back to the first principle. We might wonder why He has to repeat it. It is probably because He knows how prone we are to this failure and how much time we spend worrying about petty things that don't matter. The rebuke is growing in strength.

The Matthew 6 passage continues with,

So do not worry, saying, "What shall we eat?" or "What shall we drink?" or "What shall we wear?" For the pagans run after all these things, and your heavenly Father knows that you need them. But seek first his kingdom and his righteousness, and all these things will be given to you as well (v. 31–33).

Our lack of worry can be a strong witness. If we worry, then how are we different to non-Christians? We have a heavenly Father who loves us and knows our every need.

Verse 33 is a reminder of our priorities in life. We are not to use our emotional and physical energy worrying about things. How much better to be using our time and energy pursuing what God regards as important. That is, having priorities of holiness (becoming like Jesus), sharing our hope with others, and teaching others to trust Jesus more. Both evangelism and discipleship are difficult if we are seen to be a person who worries all the time.

* Matthew 6:34

Therefore, do not worry about tomorrow, for tomorrow will worry about itself. Each day has enough trouble of its own.

Worrying doesn't change anything. In fact, it often makes things worse because we become stressed out. As Jesus says, every day has more than enough trouble anyway.

Worrying is obviously an issue for people because there are lots of verses to do with trusting God and not worrying.

* Philippians 4:6–7

> Do not be anxious about anything, but in every situation, by prayer and petition, with thanksgiving, present your requests to God. And the peace of God, which transcends all understanding, will guard your hearts and your minds in Christ Jesus.

These verses show us how to deal with anxiety. We are to pray about everything that is troubling us. Such prayer includes asking for God's help, but it also includes thanksgiving. We need to be thanking God for His help in the past (this is part of sword fighting as we rehearse God's power in our lives in the past) and praising Him based on His character revealed in the Bible. By doing this, we are learning to thank God in advance that He is working things out and will prove trustworthy.

* Proverbs 3:5–6,

> Trust in the Lord with all your heart and lean not on your own understanding; in all your ways submit to him, and he will make your paths straight.

This verse is one that I memorized early in life and have found an immense comfort ever since. Often we make our own paths crooked (as Abraham and Sarah did in Genesis 16) because we refuse to trust God. If we would only obey Him, He would be delighted to make our paths straight.

3. Identify stories to counter this issue with Biblical truth

Here are some stories that highlight God's provision for His people.

- God provided for Noah (and all those animals) in Genesis 6–9.
- God guided Abraham as he wandered in a new country (Gen. 12–25).
- God protected Jacob as he fled from his brother and father-in-law (Gen. 28–33).
- God provided food for Elijah during a famine (1 Kings 17) and there are many, many others.

―――

Jesus was the one who called out in Matthew 11:28–30,

> Come to me, all you who are weary and burdened, and I will give you rest. Take my yoke upon you and learn from me, for I am gentle and humble in heart, and you will find rest for your souls. For my yoke is easy and my burden is light.

Being a Christian should bring times of joy and rest and if it does not, then we are probably indulging in worry. If so, we will be immeasurably adding to the stress level of our lives and failing to shine with the joy that His light yoke brings.

Reflection Questions:
1. What do you worry about?
2. Why do you worry about those particular issues?
3. How do you react to the statement that worry is a sin? Why might this be your reaction?
4. What verses of Scripture or stories from Scripture do you find particularly challenging?
5. Which particular Bible verses do you need to learn to use to fight this spiritual battle?

. . .

Prayer Suggestions:

1. Repent of anything that the Holy Spirit convicts you about.

2. Pray through some of the verses you've chosen, asking God to help you.

3. Ask God to direct you towards resources and people who can help you with this issue.

7
FEAR

Fear is part of living as created beings when things get beyond our limited control. Our fear levels are much higher if we don't know the Creator for ourselves or haven't yet learned to trust that He is in full control of all things in our world.

Fear is one of Satan's favorite weapons. Why else would the Bible repeat so often? "Do not fear."

God spoke those words to Abraham (Gen. 15:1), Isaac (Gen. 26:24), Jacob (Gen. 46:3), Joshua (numerous times but Josh. 8:1, 10:8), Daniel (Dan. 10:12), the disciples before and after His death and resurrection (John 14:1; 20:19, 26), and Paul (Acts 18:9).

I find it encouraging to know that all these heroes of the faith struggled with fear at different times. Fear is part of being human and it is something that Satan delights to play upon. Much as we try to cover our fear with laughter, bravado, or anger, it still pervades our lives.

What do we fear?

Perhaps the answer is there are many things in the world to be feared but summarized below are some categories.

1. **Fear of death**

Most people don't like to admit this but the fear of death can wield a powerful influence over us nevertheless. Abraham, and later, Isaac, both fell into this trap. This father and son, both lied about their wives, saying she was their sister, because they feared other men would kill them to take their wives (Gen. 12:10–20, 20:1–18, 26:1–11).

Their fear of death was so great, that both men allowed their wife to become a concubine to a local ruler. Rather than trust God for protection, they came up with their own plan which treated their wives as a commodity, rather than a beloved spouse.

I once knew a Taiwanese woman who was terrified of death. Wherever she went, she saw the funeral tents that are placed outside people's houses when a family member dies. This fear drove her into severe depression. She used sleeping pills to avoid her fear and slept for up to forty-eight hours at a time. Fear dominated her life and destroyed her health.

Thankfully, this fear of death also drove her into the arms of Jesus. Her fear was multiplied when her house collapsed in an earthquake. She was buried and survived, but her younger sister and brother were killed. For someone desperately afraid of death, that was almost too much and I feared that she might kill herself. She found it hard to discount the religious beliefs of her childhood which insisted that such bad luck must be caused by major sin within the family or in someone's previous incarnation.

Even though she is a Christian now, her depression continues and she often forgets to take her thoughts captive and spirals down into despair again. A few Christian friends try and stand beside her and help her with her sword fighting. They have majored on helping her think about God's love and presence and also the hope of heaven.

We talked with her about God as a loving, heavenly Father and encouraged her to meditate on stories like The Prodigal Son (Luke 15) and how much Jesus paid to give us hope and love by his death on the cross.

We helped this woman to memorize the following verses which reassured her of God's constant presence with her for all eternity.

* Hebrews 13:5

Never will I leave you, never will I forsake you.

* Or, Romans 8:31ff.,

If God is for us, who can be against us? He who did not spare his own Son...will he not also...graciously give us all things?...In all these things we are more than conquerors through him who loved us. For I am convinced that neither death nor life, neither angels nor demons, neither the present nor the future, nor any powers... nor anything else in all creation, will be able to separate us from the love of God that is in Christ Jesus our Lord.

We also taught her to reframe her situation and pointed her to a new view of death; as a door into Jesus' perfect world and presence rather than as a dreaded ending. As Psalm 56:4 says, "In God I trust and am not afraid. What can mere mortals do to me?"

We reminded her that trusting God is a sensible choice because He is fully trustworthy. With Jesus by our side, there is nothing to fear. Even if we were rejected and killed, we can still be secure for eternity.

* John 10:28

I [Jesus] give them eternal life, and they shall never perish; no one can snatch them out of my hand.

We are held in the hands of the King of the universe. Nothing can ever take us out of God's hands because He is too powerful. Although our bodies might die, we do not die but will live eternally with Jesus.

Lastly, we have spent a lot of time talking with her about heaven and how her heavenly Father is waiting for her there and as she looks into His face, there will be no room for fear. We also talk constantly about how her sister is with the Lord and that she will see her again.

When the truths of Scripture on this issue are understood, then we can be truly free of a fear of death.

I once heard of some African believers who were threatened with death if they didn't convert to Islam. One of the captured men laughed and said, "You think you can threaten me with heaven!"

When we know that even death cannot separate us from God, it no longer holds any sting (1 Cor. 15:55).

2. Fear of people

We are warned in Proverbs 29:25, "Fear of man will prove to be a snare." Sadly, this one is so common that most of us don't even recognize it. We fear losing the good opinion of others, failing in front of them, being ridiculed, or looking foolish.

Let us not be like the people mentioned in John 12:42–43,

> Many even among the leaders believed in him [Jesus]. But because of the Pharisees they would not confess their faith for fear that they would be put out of the synagogue; for they loved praise from men more than praise from God.

I would rather be like Peter and John in Acts 4 who, after being put into prison overnight and then threatened if they continued to speak about Jesus and His death and resurrection, said to the Pharisees,

> Which is right in God's eyes: to listen to you, or to him? You be the judges! As for us, we cannot help speaking about what we have seen and heard (vv. 19–20).

Our problem is that we often fear the wrong thing. We should fear only God but instead of fearing Him who has the power to determine our eternal destiny and who can judge even the thoughts and motives of our hearts, we fear people. The Old Testament in particular, talks constantly about fear of the Lord. The problem is that when people hear the word *fear* they import all their own misunderstandings about it. In the Bible, the fear of the Lord is a good thing. It is a reverence and a sense of awe at God's greatness and holiness. This fear keeps us following God's path, not because of a fear of punishment but because we know that it is the right thing to do and we long to please Him.

If we are tempted to fear people, it would be worth memorizing verses like:

* Proverbs 9:10

The fear of the Lord is the beginning of wisdom.

Why? Because it is as we fear and revere God and His holiness, and understand how He hates sin, that we will begin to get His perspective on the world. We will see fear of people as He does: an insult to Him and a lack of trust in Him. We'll realize that there is no need to fear what people can do to us (Isa. 52:12–13) but that what is important is how God views us.

In fact, wisdom could be defined as viewing things from God's perspective and thus knowing how to live our life according to His principles.

The fear of God will keep us from sinning (Exod. 2:20; Job 1:1) and helps us to live a life of balance following in God's ways (Deut. 31:12–13; Eccles. 7:16–18).

King Saul, the first king of Israel, is an example of someone who feared people more than God. In 1 Samuel 15, God had given him clear instructions how to execute His judgement on the Amalekites. He was told to kill all the men, women, and children and even all the livestock. No plunder was to be taken. But Saul did not fully obey and kept the best of the people and animals. When Samuel challenged him about his disobedience Saul said,

> "But I did obey the Lord...I went on the mission the Lord assigned me. I completely destroyed the Amalekites and brought back Agag their king. The soldiers took sheep and cattle from the plunder, the best of what was devoted to God, in order to sacrifice them to the Lord your God" (vv. 20–21).

Samuel tells Saul that God prefers obedience to sacrifice and will now reject Saul as king over Israel. Saul responds by offering the excuse,

> I was afraid of the men and so I gave in to them (v. 24).

Even Saul's repentance is dominated by the fear of people, as he begs Samuel to help him save face by coming back with him so they can worship the Lord together and make it appear as though God's favor still rests on him. Samuel rightly sees this for what it is and refuses to be part of it.

How often have we done the wrong thing because we were more afraid of what others think than what God thinks?

Emily was a keen Christian who really wanted to serve the Lord. However, over the course of the week she was staying with me, I noticed that she seemed to be full of fear that was crippling her. On further questioning, I discovered that she was also bound by low self-esteem and worry. Thankfully, although this seemed like three different issues, they were all linked.

I discovered through gentle questioning that Emily was afraid of many things. She was afraid of failure and incompetence (this severely affected her ability to minister to others and try new things). She was afraid of rejection (this severely affected her ability to share the gospel with friends). She was afraid of the future both for herself and for her family. The list could have gone on and on. Thankfully, understanding how the sword worked, I knew that I didn't need to deal with every fear separately. I explained to her the principles of sword fighting and then how to use her sword.

Apart from many of the verses noted in the rest of this chapter, Emily also wrote down:

* Psalm 46:1–2

> God is our refuge and strength, an ever present help in trouble. Therefore, we will not fear, though the earth give way and the mountains fall into the heart of the sea...

We don't have to fear because of the One that we trust in. No matter what happens, He is more than able to be our refuge and strength. There are hundreds of similar verses that you might choose and here are some of them.

* Romans 8:28–29

> We know that in all things God works for the good of those who have been called according to his purpose [and this purpose is]...to be conformed to the image of his Son.

This promise is not that all things will turn out for good. Instead, it is a promise that if we trust God, He will use everything including our failures and sufferings to make us more like Jesus. With this kind of God, what is there to fear?

* Isaiah 41:10

> So do not fear, for I am with you; do not be dismayed, for I am your God. I will strengthen you and help you; I will uphold you with my righteous right hand.

God promises to give us all we need to go through life's fears. We just need to trust Him.

* 1 John 4:18

There is no fear in love. But perfect love drives out fear, because fear has to do with punishment. The one who fears is not made perfect in love.

There is enough in this verse to keep us meditating for ages. One solution to our fear is to think repeatedly about God's love. If He loved us enough to die for us, then He is not going to forget about us or fail to give us everything we need. We will never outgrow the need to go over the basics of the gospel of Jesus. The more we are aware of God's love for us, the less we will fear.

This verse should also be a stimulus for us to keep on loving others with God's love. For as we do, our fear about our relationships will decrease.

* The stories of Peter (John 18:15ff., 18:25ff.; 21:15ff.) or John Mark[1] remind us that failure is not final. God is the God of second chances. There is no need to fear failure because God can use it to achieve His purposes. We only fail if we refuse to submit to God. God can redeem failure and then use us to comfort others with the comfort we have received (2 Cor. 1:3–4).

Emily adapted the methods I suggested to suit herself. She chose one verse at a time and memorized it, then recited that one verse for a whole week. In the second week, she went on to the second verse and so on.

Results can occur far more quickly that we might expect. On the second morning of her new sword fighting regime, Emily suddenly sat up in bed and said, "I'm not scared. For the first morning of my life, I'm not scared to face the day!"

Exciting as this was, it was not the signal to put down the sword and let it rust again. It is merely a signal that God is keeping His promises, and that sword fighting is God's way of overcoming our fears and anxieties.

I have kept up with Emily via email. She reports steady and exciting progress. Sometimes she doesn't fight and so backslides into a short period of giving in to Satan's lies. However, once she has used her sword again, Satan flees and she experiences victory. She is radically changed from the woman I first knew. She is no longer controlled by her fears, but is free to serve and glorify God. She is now a missionary, which is something she wouldn't have dared to do before she learnt to sword fight.

3. Fear of the future

One of the interesting things about fear is that Satan often makes us fear things that haven't happened yet. We fear that if we say such and such, we will be laughed at or rejected. We fear that if we do something, then we'll fail or it will turn out badly.

Many of the things we fear about the future, never even happen. However, it doesn't matter whether they do or not, if Satan can convince us to fear, then he has succeeded and we feel as miserable as if the consequences had occurred. Sometimes our fear is what leads to the very consequence that we were trying to avoid.

C. H. Spurgeon once said,

> Such strange creatures are we that, we probably smart more under blows which never fall upon us than we do under those which do actually come. The rod of God does not smite us as sharply as the rod of our own imagination does; our groundless fears are our chief tormentors.[2]

When I left Australia to become a missionary, there were many things that I feared. Major fears were that I would fail to do a good job and would have to return in disgrace and embarrassment. I also feared that I would hate being a missionary (after preparing for it much of my life). As I was going to the same country where my parents had been missionaries, I feared that I would be compared unfavorably with them.

The last stop before Taiwan was to spend four weeks at our international headquarters in Singapore. One talk stopped me in my tracks. A Chinese Singaporean lady spoke about fear and boldly said, "Fear is a sin."[3] The minute I heard that sentence my thoughts screamed in protest and I thought, "But everybody is scared, it's not really so bad is it?"

The speaker went on to say, "Fear is a sin because it is a failure to trust God." As I thought about it, I realized the speaker was right. When I fear, I am essentially saying to God, "You're not in control, you can't sort out this situation and you need my help!" How presumptuous I was! Realizing that fear is a sin was my first step in being willing to face it and start dealing with it. If we think of fear as just a minor foible, then we are unlikely to tackle it head on. Satan wants us to dismiss this idea of fear being sin because then he can defeat us in this area. So the first thing we need to do is repent and apologize for refusing to trust God.

I then went on to remind myself of many of the verses in this chapter. Since then, whenever I am tempted to fear the future, I jump on the situation quickly, repent, choose to trust and go forward. My mother wrote out Proverbs 3:5–6 in my Bible as a little girl and it is still one of my favorites: "Trust in the Lord with all your heart and lean not on your own understanding. In all your ways acknowledge him and he will direct your paths."[4] It is so comforting for me to remember that my understanding is limited, but God's is infinite. He delights in directing my paths and is more than capable of doing it without my help or interference!

The next chapter focuses on a particular fear that we all struggle with (i.e. the fear of doing evangelism). It will allow us a chance to work through a complete, concrete example. In the meantime, you might like to reflect on the following.

Reflection Questions:
1. What do you fear and why?
2. How does the fact that the Bible tells us so often "do not fear" encourage you?
3. Which Biblical story particularly speaks to your fears?
4. Which verses speak to your fears?

· · ·

Prayer Suggestions:
    1. Turn your fears over to the Lord.
    2. Repent of your fears and ask for courage.
    3. Turn the verses and stories into prayer.

---

1. John Mark dropped out of Paul and Barnabus' first missionary journey (Acts 15:36–39) and was later the cause of division between Paul and Barnabus. Yet, he went on to author the Gospel of Mark and Paul said of him in later life, "he is helpful to me" (2 Tim. 4:11).
2. A sermon called "Needless Fears" preached on, 11 June, 1874. https://www.biblebb.com/files/spurgeon/3098.htm
3. Mary Tay, March, 1999.
4. *New International Version* (Grand Rapids: Zondervan, 1978).

8

FEAR IN EVANGELISM

Satan is clever at making us believe that we are the only ones who struggle with something. When we feel alone and isolated, we quickly become discouraged and give up.

This isolation is noticeable when we seek to share our faith with someone else. Our thoughts might include:

- What if they ask me a tough question and I can't answer? I'll feel like a fool.
- They might reject me if I share about Jesus. Go slowly, and maybe they can just be won over by my deeds.

This temptation is particularly powerful because it contains some half-truths. Yes, our deeds are important, but the problem is that without explaining why we are good, loving and so on, our friend might assume we are a good Buddhist or just a nice person. A combination of good deeds and clear communication is far more effective.

- I'm feeling tired now. Why not wait until tomorrow?

- This is not my particular gifting. Why don't I leave it to someone else who is better at evangelism?
- I'm at work. It's better to wait until a more suitable time and place.

And so on.

When I first open my mouth, I am assailed by strong doubt that the person really needs to hear the gospel. I struggle the most when the person is nice and seems to be doing okay as they are.

We often assume, incorrectly, that real evangelists don't struggle with these thoughts. We begin to reason that if we have these kinds of thoughts, it must prove that we aren't really suitable for evangelism.

I have been consistently doing evangelism since 1996. Never once have I not been fearful before I open my mouth. The difference is that I have learnt that these thoughts are normal and I have learned how to use my sword.

With practice, I have learnt to sword fight so quickly that within a few seconds, I will open my mouth. Once I take that first step, I discover that all God's promises are true and that He gives me all the resources I need. I am often encouraged by the words that God gives me to share because I know that they are His wisdom not my own.

Throughout an evangelistic conversation, I am continually having to use my sword. The stronger the mental battle, the more I am inspired to continue because the intensity of the battle shows me that Satan is afraid of what I am doing.

Here are some of the verses and principles that I review at different stages of any evangelistic opportunity.

Before the gospel conversation
* 1 Peter 2:9

You are a chosen people...that you may declare the praises of him who called you out of darkness into his wonderful light.

* 1 Peter 3:15

Always be prepared to give an answer to everyone who asks you to give the reason for the hope that you have.

When I am tempted to think that evangelism is for someone else to do, then I remind myself of these two verses that point out that we are all meant to share our hope and the blessings of being a child of God.

If I don't feel like sharing, then I spend time just reminding myself of how wonderful it is to be a Christian. That quickly makes me want to tell others about Jesus so that they can share in the blessings I have received. This is why it is so important for us to be preaching the gospel to ourselves. Reminding ourselves of the wonder of our salvation is one way to actually put on the helmet of salvation. Another practical way is to remind ourselves of the realities of hell. I find this particularly helpful when I am tempted not to tell the gospel to nice people. I remind myself of why Jesus said He was the only way to salvation and that hell is real.

* When I am tempted to put off sharing until tomorrow, I remind myself that life is short and uncertain and like the rich fool in Luke 12:16ff. any of us might die and have to face God.

* I also remind myself of how terrible it would be on Judgement Day if any of my friends turned to me and said, "Why didn't you ever tell me about Jesus?" I don't want to shoulder the responsibility of their blood on my head (Ezek. 33).

* I remind myself of how God delights to use the weak (1 Cor. 1:27–29) and how He will give me all the resources I need (Luke 21:15), even in the toughest circumstances.

* If I am rejected, I recall verses that assure me that God is with me and will never forsake me (Heb. 13:5; Rom 8:31ff.).

During the gospel conversation

I have thoughts like, "Oh, that was poorly said," or "That sounds ridiculous, do you really believe that?"

Talking about Jesus with cult members is particularly difficult. I often find myself thinking, "You're just wasting your time. People like this won't change." I also end up feeling foolish because they quote the Bible so confidently.

* I constantly remind myself that God can still do His work even though I do a poor job because He is not limited by my poor communication skills. Think of Jonah who reluctantly preached eight words. His attitude is not one to emulate. Jonah hated the Ninevites and wanted God to wipe them out. Despite the messenger's attitude, God worked through his words and brought a whole city of Ninevites to repentance.

* Isaiah 55:11

> [God's word] will not return to me empty but will accomplish what I desire.

As long as it is God's word that I am sharing, then I can be confident that it will accomplish what God desires whether it is salvation or judgement. This is certainly a promise that God will achieve His purposes. I am not sure (as some say) that this guarantees people who hear the gospel message will become believers.

* Romans 1:16

> I am not ashamed of the gospel, because it is the power of God that brings salvation to everyone who believes...

No matter how foolish the gospel sometimes sounds when I share it, I keep quoting this verse silently to myself. We should never give up, God is more than able to save anyone.

* I remind myself that all people need the gospel and that sharing it is never a waste of time. Maybe something I say will be used by God to start the non-Christian on a search for God. Or, it may be nothing I say but simply the manner in which I relate to them.

After the gospel conversation

Doing evangelism is the time when the spiritual battle is most evident to me. The battle is unrelenting and requires constant prayer and repetition of Scriptures. We fight this battle at the same time as we're trying to listen and respond appropriately. No wonder we feel tired afterwards.

After a gospel conversation, our enemy doesn't give up. He either bombards us with thoughts of "That was terrible and you wasted your time," or the opposite, "That went well and didn't you do a good job!"

Both responses require us to continue the sword fight.

* I remind myself of the concepts in 1 Corinthians 3:5–7. Although each of us has a different role in evangelism, such as prayer or sharing, it is only God who brings growth and life. Without Christ we are spiritually dead (Eph. 2:1). No matter how brilliant a communicator I am, the raising of the dead is always the work of God. Remembering this keeps me humble.

It also helps me to fight discouragement because I realize that my role is as a sower of the word of God (Mark 4), but it is God who causes the seed to sprout and grow.

When we learn to fight with our sword during evangelism, we begin to rely totally on God's leading and strength. It is a process that really helps us grow. The more evangelism we do, the more we are able to use past experiences of God's help and wisdom as part of the fight. That means, we are able to remember how often we have felt scared and inadequate, and yet, God has proved more than able to help us in any and every situation.

The whole process is like exercising. I have kept fit since 1995, but I seldom feel like going out to exercise. I am only able to do so because I remind myself of the positive benefits of exercise and how it makes me feel. That spurs me on.

Reminding myself of all the experiences I have had sharing the gospel gives me the motivation to open my mouth.

. . .

Reflection Questions:

1. What do you fear when you see an opportunity to share your faith?

2. What were your previous responses to these fears? Did they work, why or why not?

3. Choose a list of suitable Bible verses and principles and start practicing with your sword.

4. Once you see progress, share what you have learned with someone else.

Prayer Suggestions:

1. Ask God to help you focus on Him.

2. Spend time praising God for His greatness and for our marvelous salvation.

3. Pray that you'll learn to listen more to Jesus and His truth, than your fears.

9
DOUBT

Doubt has been one of the most effective weapons of the enemy since the Garden of Eden.

In Genesis 3, the snake asks Eve,

Did God really say you must not eat from any tree in the garden?

We all know that God had only prohibited the eating of one kind of fruit. Why then did the snake ask such a question? Was it an attempt to check up on whether Eve was clear on God's instructions and to make Eve doubt the goodness of God? It is almost like the snake is saying, "Well, isn't God a bit unreasonable and mean? God is not after your best interests. He's holding out on you."

Doubt often raises the question of whether God really cares and whether He is truly good.

Many of the heroes of the faith have been tempted in this area.

Abraham was seventy-five years old when God promised to make him the father of a nation. He knew this would not happen without him having a son (Gen. 12:1–7). By the time he was eighty-five, is it any wonder he and Sarah had begun to doubt? Their doubts drove them to use the culturally accepted way to have a son—using a second wife or concubine (Gen. 16). Their decision to go their own way instead of trusting God, led to years of family conflict and a world conflict that has been going on for nearly 4000 years.

Jacob fled from his older twin brother, Esau (Gen. 27–33). He must have doubted he would ever be blessed and be able to return to Canaan.

As Joseph languished in slavery and prison, he must have been tempted to doubt God's goodness to him and that his visions would come true (Gen. 37–50).

The Israelites must surely have doubted whether God could hear their prayers or cared enough to rescue them while they were slaves in Egypt. Did God really have the power to rescue them or would they be slaves forever (Exod. 6:9)?

All through the wilderness years, the Israelites often doubted that God had the strength and ability to rescue them from their enemies, and from hunger and thirst (Num. 14, 20). Even after He had brought them to the promised land they often went their own way and refused to let God be king (1 Sam. 8). They preferred to worship gods they could see rather than an invisible God (Exod. 32). When the promised Savior came, they ignored and doubted all evidence that he was God and crucified Him.

1. Doubting God's goodness and power

Has there ever been anyone in all of history who has not been tempted to doubt God's goodness and/or His power to help? When anything bad happens to us, we cry out "Why me?" It is all too easy to believe that God does not care, that He does not see us, or that He is powerless.

Each of us has areas where we are vulnerable: parents longing for a child who never comes, a single person longing for a spouse, someone suffering chronic pain or weakness, people struggling with unemployment, someone dealing with domestic violence or alcoholism or gambling. The list of our vulnerabilities is extensive.

As our pain and struggle goes on and on, it is easy to question whether we are being punished by God or simply forgotten.

Here are some of the verses and principles that can be used to fight this battle in the arena of doubt.

* We need to remind ourselves of the power and sovereignty of God. Our God is the God who made the universe (Gen. 1; Ps. 8).

* We should also remind ourselves of the goodness and love of God who died for us. Will He not give us all things (Rom. 8:32)?

* Psalm 55:22

> Cast your cares on the Lord and he will sustain you; he will never let the righteous be shaken.

* Romans 8:28–29

> We know that in all things God works for the good of those who have been called according to his purpose [and this purpose is]...to be conformed to the image of his Son.

God is not primarily interested in making our lives smooth and easy but in making us more mature. EVERY circumstance can be used by God to make us more like Jesus.

* Reflect on the stories of those who suffered but continued to trust. Good examples are those of Joseph (Gen. 37–50) and Job.

* If you struggle with contentment in the life situation that God has given you, remind yourself of stories or passages that focus on God being the one to provide all the security, love and acceptance that we need. Perhaps the passage when Jesus said,

> I am the bread of life. Whoever comes to me will never go hungry, and whoever believes in me will never be thirsty (John 6:35).

Having experienced a more Middle Eastern culture where bread is the main sustenance and is present at every meal, I can better grasp what Jesus was saying. He was claiming to be the main satisfying food, without which the people did not feel full. Bread for the Jewish culture two thousand years ago was like rice to the Chinese and potatoes to the Irish. Without it, you didn't feel full or that you had really eaten. We need to remind ourselves that Jesus claimed to be the only satisfaction and claim that promise by leaning completely on Him. The more we lean on Him, the more we will find that He is trustworthy.

2. Doubting the truth of the gospel

I was once asked to counsel a university student who, after being a Christian for several years, was having severe doubts about the truths of the gospel. She had begun to wonder if she'd believed in a lie. I met with her several times and went through the evidence for believing in the historicity of the Bible records and the resurrection. I tried to deal with each doubt that she had. I'm not convinced that my counsel did much good because I hadn't learnt many of the lessons in this book.

If I had the time again, I would encourage her to memorize and review the verses that summarize the gospel twice daily. I would include:

a) God's character and creation
* Revelation 4:11

You are worthy, our Lord and God, to receive glory and honor and power, for you created all things, and by your will they were created and have their being.

* Psalm 19:1–2

The heavens declare the glory of God; the skies proclaim the work of his hands. Day after day they pour forth speech; night after night they reveal knowledge.

b) Our rebellion and main problem

* Jeremiah 17:9

The heart is deceitful above all things and beyond cure.

* Romans 3:10–11

There is no one righteous, not even one. There is no one who seeks God...

* Romans 3:23

All have sinned and fall short of the glory of God.

c) Who Jesus claims to be
  * Go through some stories declaring his authority over sickness (Mark 5:21ff.), demons (Mark 5:1–20), nature (Mark 4:35–41), sin (Mark 2:1–12), and death (John 11).
  * Also go through the "I am" statements that Jesus makes about Himself in the book of John in their context. (Bread (John 6:35), Light (John 8:12), Door (John 10:7ff.), Shepherd (John 10:11ff.), Way, Truth, Life (John 14:6), Vine (John 15:1, 5)).

d) Why Jesus had to die and rise and what His death achieved

Although I did not know about sword fighting when I was asked to meet with the student mentioned earlier, by accident I hit on another application of the same principle. Rather than having her review Bible verses, I suggested that she and a keen Christian friend find some non-Christians with whom they could run some sort of course to examine the gospel. She did this and I was surprised how quickly her doubts resolved. As she was forced to face non-Christian classmates' questions, she had to review the gospel and evidence for herself. She also re-read all four Gospels. The constant reiteration of the truths of the gospel led her to believe it once again for herself.

Ever since that time, if I have found a person doubting the gospel,

I have suggested that they become involved in evangelism as part of the solution to the problem.

3. Doubting God's power

Rather than going through individual verses, it is worthwhile following the examples in Scripture. At times when the Israelites were facing new challenges or difficulties, their leaders reminded everyone of God's great power through their history. For example, the whole book of Deuteronomy is Moses reviewing their history before he dies and Joshua will take over leading the people into the Promised Land. Samuel does the same kind of revision when Saul is anointed king and Samuel wants them to focus on God, not an earthly king (1 Sam. 12:6ff.).

Other stories we can consider is the account of creation from Genesis (meditating on how amazing it is), the Exodus (Exod. 1–20), the Gospels and Acts.

4. Doubting that God answers prayer

Sometimes we can doubt that God hears us because we don't see the results of prayer right away or He doesn't answer in the way we expect. There may be several reasons for this.

a) God is answering, but not in our time frame

There are many stories and passages about delayed answers to prayer. For example, in Exodus, God does not immediately rescue the Israelites from slavery. Even when he does send Moses as a rescuer, God doesn't save His people immediately. Indeed, they still have to endure ten plagues and their consequences.

Why might God have taken so long to answer? Did God have a hearing problem or a poor memory? Or was it because He had a greater plan which included rescuing some of the Egyptians? During the seventh plague (Exod. 9:13–28) some of the Egyptians avoided the plague of hail because they had learned to fear the Lord. Reverence for God meant that when they heard the warning about the coming plague, they hurried to bring their slaves and livestock inside under cover.

Exodus 9:15–16 also tells us clearly what God was working to achieve.

> For by now I could have stretched out my hand and struck you and your people with a plague that would have wiped you off the earth. But I have raised you up for this very purpose, that I might show you my power and that my name might be proclaimed in all the earth.

God didn't just want to rescue the Israelites but He planned to rescue some Egyptians and other people further afield. We know that Rahab trusted God because of the plagues in Egypt (Joshua 2:9–11) and the Gibeonites did as well (Josh. 9:24–25).

In our situation, when God is telling us to wait, could it be that He has a greater plan?

b) God says "No" because our prayers are selfish

Another reason our prayers aren't answered is that we pray selfish prayers that are not according to His will. God doesn't give in to our silly requests any more than a good father would give his two-year-old a sharp knife just because the child asks for it. If I ask God to give me something that will ultimately harm me and my relationship with God, why should I be angry when He refuses?

c) Our prayers aren't specific enough

Sometimes our prayers are vague. The "God bless Granny" kinds of prayers mean that it is difficult to know when they have been answered. I learned to make more specific prayers by keeping a prayer diary. I listed the date I started praying and noted the date the request was answered with a "yes" or "no." I learned a lot by pondering why God answered the way He did. I also learned the kind of prayers that God delighted to answer and so I started praying more of those.

Thus, the way to deal with the doubt that God answers prayers is to study the Biblical stories and to stretch ourselves in learning to pray the kinds of prayers that God delights to answer.

· · ·

Reflection Questions:

1. What areas of God's word or character are you tempted to doubt?

2. Which particular verses or principles could you use to counter those doubts? Record them and review them often.

Prayer Suggestions:

1. Repent of your doubts

2. Praise God for His trustworthiness and character.

3. Pray in response to the verses you chose. Ask God to help you trust Him.

4. Start a prayer diary.

10
GUILT

King David was a man whose emotions have been laid out for all to see. The psalms that he wrote have been public property for 3000 years. He'd served God faithfully for decades when he committed adultery with Bathsheba and arranged for the murder of her husband, Uriah, to cover up his sin, yet he seemed to feel no guilt. What self-deception! It was not until God sent the prophet Nathan to tell David a story, that David experienced any guilt. Healthy guilt pushes us towards repentance (2 Sam. 12).

We are blessed to have David's prayer of repentance recorded for us in Psalm 51. This is a brutally honest prayer. A prayer that is far from the false repentance of simply saying sorry because David wants to feel better, or one that is trying to manipulate God into reducing the consequences of sin. It is the prayer of a man who can see the depth of his sin.

Despite having sinned against Uriah, Bathsheba, the people of Israel, and his unborn child, David can see that ultimately all sin is a direct rebellion against God. This is clearly shown when he says,

Against you, you only, have I sinned and done what is evil in your sight (Ps. 51:4).

He approaches God, not as the king of Israel, but as a sinful man who has nothing good to offer God and must cry out for God's undeserved mercy. He acknowledges that God is perfectly justified in judging him. Only when David has spoken of his own wickedness, does he beg God for forgiveness. He knows that being cut off from the presence of God would be the ultimate punishment (Ps. 51:11). He acknowledges that God won't be impressed with a show of religious ritual, but only with heartfelt sorrow, confession and humility (Ps. 51:16–17).

Our conscience is a strange thing. It was given to us by God to help us discern the difference between right and wrong, but we seem to have different sensitivities to its guidance (Rom. 2:15). We can ignore our conscience and the more we do, the more insensitive it becomes. We see this in David's case where even adultery and murder don't seem to have troubled his conscience. Alternatively, we can be oversensitive and begin to feel guilty where there is no guilt or even feel guilty about the wrong thing and in doing so be oblivious to where the real sin lies.

Our enemy does not give up. He loves to convince us that our sin is too big for God to forgive (and thus, that we will have to live with our guilt), so we don't truly repent. Or after we have repented, he likes to keep reminding us of our sin so that we continue to feel guilty.

We make things easier for Satan because so many of us have false views of God. We picture God either as a terrifying, condemning judge or, as so loving and accommodating of us and our foibles, that there is no need for repentance.

These contrasting images contain enough truth about our God to be powerful lies and both of them achieve Satan's purposes of causing us to fail to deal with our guilt. Yes, God is loving, but it is not a wishy-washy love of not caring about our sin or accepting it as unimportant. Rather, it is the love that saw Jesus take our punishment upon Himself, dealing with it once and for all for eternity. And yes, God is a judge and He will be terrifying for those who don't know Him. But, for those of us who are His children, His judgement and love come together to warmly welcome and forgive us.

More than fifteen years ago, I was part of a short-term mission team, sent to the outer islands of Taiwan. I was assigned a room with one of the local Taiwanese team members. In the morning, I enquired politely how she had slept. She told me that she had slept poorly but that she always did, because she had such terrible nightmares.

I was prompted to ask her how long she had been having this problem and she said it had been eight years. I immediately asked her what had happened eight years before. She told me that she had committed a sin that God couldn't forgive.

I continued to ask questions and to pray, asking God to show me what was really happening. She said that initially she had only had nightmares, but soon fears and other issues multiplied in her life. First, she started to sleep with the light on, which disturbed both her own and her husband's sleep. Then she moved the children into her bedroom to make herself feel more secure and this obviously affected her relationship with her husband.

Then I said to her, "I am guessing that your children have all sorts of fears, like fear of the dark." She wondered how I knew this and I pointed out that she had indirectly taught her children to be fearful.

By the time I met her, this lady was ensnared by fear, feelings of hopelessness, and low self-esteem, to the extent that she couldn't even share about Jesus with anyone. She had hoped that coming on a local outreach might solve these problems. I explained that the solution to her problem was to deal with the original issue; namely, that she believed she had committed a sin that God couldn't forgive.

After talking about the sword of the Spirit, we started to think about what God's word said about forgiveness. Here are some of the verses we shared.

* 1 John 1:9

> If we confess our sins, he is faithful and just and will forgive us our sins and purify us from all unrighteousness.

I asked her to read the verse out and tell me what it said. I asked her if she'd confessed her sin and she said that she had done so many times but never felt she had been forgiven. I asked her again what the verse said. Again she told me and I asked her whether she wanted to believe Satan's accusations ("God could never forgive me for that sin.") or God's word ("...will forgive us our sins and purify us from all unrighteousness")?

* Psalm 103:12

> As far as the east is from the west, so far has he removed our transgressions from us.

We discussed this verse in depth and she realized that not only would God forgive her, but that He would never bring the issue up again. Even if she committed the same sin again, God will still forgive her just as He did the first time. Thus, if the sin kept coming up, it wasn't God bringing it up.

* We talked about the principles found in Hebrews of "once for all" (Heb. 10:1–14) which meant that Jesus' death was more than sufficient to cleanse her sin.

* We briefly talked about the nature of the sin that cannot be forgiven (Matt. 12:31) and I assured her that if she desired to be forgiven, then she couldn't have committed that unforgivable sin!

Because this lady had chosen to believe Satan's lies in one area of her life, those lies had begun to spread and influence other parts of her life. Having dealt with the root issue (doubting God's word about forgiveness and her subsequent false guilt), we were easily able to deal with the overflow—the fear issue in her life. For the first time in many years, she slept well and the next day had the courage to share her faith.

Susan ended up pregnant before marriage. Although, she had repented of the issues related to pre-marital sex, she was plagued by continuing guilt. This guilt began to affect her relationship with her fiancé and her attitude to her unborn child. In addition, she felt cut off from God and continually berated herself for her failure.

After discussing the background to sword fighting we came up with these verses and ideas.

* Luke 15:11–32

We talked about the parable of the Prodigal Son and the kind of father that God is. I wanted her to be assured that God is always waiting for us to come home and that He welcomes us back without any accusation or even an "I told you so," but instead with joy, acceptance, and love.

We reviewed God's promises to forgive and remove our sin. (See above as well as 1 John 1:9 and Ps. 103:12).

Then we spent time discussing why Satan would want her to feel guilty and believe that God had not forgiven her. We talked through the implications of believing Satan's lies and how destructive it would be to her marriage, her relationship with her children, church and so on.

Other passages that could be considered with someone like Susan could include:

* Romans 8:31–34

If God is for us, who can be against us? He who did not spare his own Son, but gave him up for us all—how will he not also, along with him, graciously give us all things? Who will bring any charge against those God has chosen? It is God who justifies. Who then is the one that condemns?

It is because of the death and resurrection of Jesus that we can be forgiven for our sins. His death dealt with the universal problem of sin and its effects such as death, guilt, and being under the power of sin and others.

* 2 Corinthians 1:3b–4

> ...the God of all comfort, who comforts us in all our troubles, so that we can comfort those in any trouble with the comfort we ourselves receive from God.

Finally, we discussed how God can bring good even out of our sin. What she had learnt through her moral failure could be turned into ministry in the future. God doesn't waste our past but transforms us and allows it to be used to warn and encourage others. These verses gave her great hope in the place of her despair.

The fight with false guilt is seldom a once off situation as Satan usually keeps bringing up issues again but thankfully the solution is always the same. Just like Susan, we need to remind ourselves of the forgiveness that was won for us by Jesus' death on the cross; and remind ourselves of God's promises, choosing to believe them.

Many people certainly feel ongoing guilt for the lives they led before becoming Christians. Did Paul struggle with this? He had severely persecuted Christians before his conversion on the Damascus Road. He must have struggled with guilt as Satan tried to sabotage his effectiveness in ministry.

Some other verses that might help someone deal with such guilt include:

* Psalm 130:3–4

If you Lord, kept a record of sins, Lord, who could stand? But with you there is forgiveness, so that we can, with reverence, serve you.

* Romans 8:1–2

Therefore, there is now no condemnation for those who are in Christ Jesus, because through Christ Jesus the law of the Spirit who gives life has set you free from the law of sin and death.

* 1 Corinthians 6:11

And that is what some of you were. But you were washed, you were sanctified, you were justified in the name of the Lord Jesus Christ and by the Spirit of God.

* Ephesians 3:12

In him and through faith in him we may approach God with freedom and confidence.

* Hebrews 10:22

Let us draw near to God with a sincere heart and with the full assurance that faith brings, having our hearts sprinkled to cleanse us from a guilty conscience and having our bodies washed with pure water.

Reflection Questions:
1. Do you have sins that you have sought forgiveness for but Satan keeps reminding you about? How has that affected your life?
2. What verses or principles would most help your situation? Record them and start using them in your sword fighting.

. . .

Prayer Suggestions:
1. Repent of your failure to believe God's promises.

2. Thank Jesus for His salvation and ask for strength to keep trusting God's word.

11
IMPURITY

If you wanted to look at pornography forty years ago, it took money and effort. With the Internet, mobile phones, and even free-to-air television and advertising, we are now bombarded with pornographic images. It is almost impossible to avoid them.

From pornography, or even the flesh-exposing clothes seen in public, it is an easy slide into fantasy. The more we allow our thoughts to dwell on impure things, the more easily our thoughts can be translated into action.

Once again, King David's story is a clear example of this. King David was a "man after God's own heart" (1 Sam. 13:14), yet he ended up committing adultery and then arranging for the murder of Bathsheba's husband to cover up his sin.

How could someone fall so far away from God's standards of behavior? Like most stories of this kind of immorality, it didn't happen all at once. If you had asked David when he was a young man if he would become an adulterer and murderer, he would have replied with a shocked, "Never!" Sin started with small steps that led to compromises and a gradual slide away from God until at last the "impossible" happened.

In David's case, it seems that he was not doing his duty as a king in leading his men in battle (2 Sam. 11:1). He had too much spare time and instead of using his time wisely, he spent it wandering around his rooftop. He must have known that from his (presumably higher) rooftop he could see women bathing. Once he'd seen Bathsheba, he progressed to thinking about her, then enquiring about who she was. Then he misused his power and sent for her and slept with her. At any point he could have rejected the temptation, but instead he slid further and further from God's principles. Eventually, Bathsheba became pregnant and David tried to cover it up by getting her husband, Uriah, to come home. But Uriah was too righteous a man to return home to his wife when none of the other soldiers could return home.

David was so desperate to get Uriah to sleep with his wife, and thus be able to pretend that the baby was not his, that he got Uriah drunk. Even drunk, Uriah honored God and refused to go home to his wife.

David took the final slide away from God, by asking his general to arrange for Uriah to be killed. Then David married Bathsheba quickly, before she was obviously pregnant and people started to do the math (v. 27).

David had so deadened his conscience that when the prophet, Nathan, was sent to confront him, the story Nathan told (which seems so obvious to us) didn't even connect with David's conscience. It never occurred to him that Nathan was talking about him. Instead, David glibly said, "The man who did this deserves to die!" It was not until Nathan said, "You are the man" (2 Sam. 12:7) that David realized that what he had done was both wicked and a total denial of his status as a child of God.

David's story resonates because there are so many others who have done similar things, at least in terms of impurity and adultery. All I have spoken with will attest that the sin started in their thoughts, then gradually its impact spread, until they eventually acted upon their thoughts.

I wish I only had a single story to illustrate this one but sadly, all of us can probably list numerous instances of this kind of sin. Sin that starts with impurity, fantasy, and then moves towards the sexual act. Along the way, this kind of sin can be entangled with the objectivization of other people and violence.

The steps for other sexual sins are similar: from the eyes, to the thoughts, to the actions.

Satan would love to convince us that "This couldn't happen to me." Don't fall into that trap.

This sin devastates families and ministries, and brings huge dishonor to God and so it needs to be dealt with from the first thought. Don't let us deceive ourselves that we are in control and can limit ourselves to only thinking about such things.

Every new Christian who is discipled should be taught how to deal with impurity. We might feel a little embarrassed to raise such an issue, but it must be done to safeguard ourselves and God's reputation. When a Christian falls into sin in this area, it has a major impact on others. Christians become discouraged and disappointed and non-Christians use it to mock Christians and say, "See, you're just the same (or worse, because you claim to be better) than us."

With all the issues mentioned in this book, an accountability partner would be of immense help. This is especially true with the issue of impurity. We need to find someone we can trust who will ask us tough questions about how we're going in this area. Both people need each other's prayers and both need help to keep accountable in sword fighting.

Some helpful things to meditate on could include:

* Lots of reflection on the character of God as a holy God. Exodus 19 is a key passage about the holiness of God and the importance of fearing Him as we treat Him with the respect He deserves. The more we understand the holiness of God, the more we won't dare to indulge in impure thoughts or behavior. As we get closer to God, "the consuming fire" (Deut. 4:24; Heb. 12:29), the dross of our impurities will be burnt away.

* Matthew 5:27–29

> You have heard that it was said, "You shall not commit adultery." But I tell you that anyone who looks at a woman lustfully has already committed adultery with her in his heart. If your right eye causes you to stumble, gouge it out and throw it away. It is better for you to lose one part of your body than for your whole body to be thrown into hell.

These verses remind us how seriously God takes not only adultery but lust. We are to spring into action and take every thought captive, rather than to dwell on impure things. It is lust that is the root problem. If we don't deal with lust, then increased impurity and even adultery is almost inevitable without God's gracious intervention. We must be ruthless with lust and dig that sin out before it grows.

* It is not only God who is holy but we are told repeatedly that He has chosen us to be holy (Lev. 11:44; 1 Cor. 3:17; Eph. 1:4; Col. 1:22). That is, we are set apart to be pure; to be different from everyone around us in thoughts and speech. Pure thoughts, pure words, and pure actions. We could also think about the consequences of failing in this area, in terms of the non-Christians we might prevent coming to Christ because of our poor witness and the dishonor we would bring on Jesus' name.

Perhaps meditate on a verse like 1 Peter 2:9, that reminds us of our status and the reason that might prevent us drifting into impurity. We have a high calling to live up to.

> You are a chosen people, a royal priesthood, a holy nation, a people belonging to God, that you may declare the praises of him who called you out of darkness into his wonderful light.

* 1 Peter 1:18–19

For you know that it was not with perishable things such as silver or gold that you were redeemed from the empty way of life handed down to you from your ancestors, but with the precious blood of Christ, a lamb without blemish or defect.

The more we meditate on what our redemption cost God, the more we would be ashamed and reluctant to treat that sacrifice casually.

* 1 Corinthians 6:18–20

Flee from sexual immorality. All other sins a person commits are outside the body, but whoever sins sexually, sins against their own body. Do you not know that your bodies are temples of the Holy Spirit, who is in you, whom you have received from God? You are not your own; you were bought at a price. Therefore honor God with your bodies.

These are the final words in a long argument that Paul gives for being sexually pure. He argues that when we are sexually involved with someone, we become one. To do this with anyone other than a spouse is to unite not only yourself but also God (since the Holy Spirit lives in us) with this person. The thought should disgust us.

Paul also argues that sexual immorality is one sin that harms even our bodies. We shouldn't need the statistics for pregnancy, abortion, sexual disease, and the psychological effects, to convince us of this. Sexual immorality cannot be indulged in casually because God designed sex to work best within a loving marriage. We ignore the Creator's instructions at our cost.

Our body is also to be used in pure ways because it is the dwelling place of God's spirit. We should clothe it and use it in ways that bring glory to God.

* Ephesians 4:22–5:20 urges us to take off anything that is from our old nature and instead to put on the new. Part of this is sexual impurity, obscenity, and coarse or lewd joking. Anything that is unwholesome will not only harm us and direct our thoughts to impurity, but it will encourage others to follow in the same way. Instead, we are urged to "put on" any kind of helpful talk that will "build others up" and may "benefit those who listen" (Eph. 4:29).

Imagine what a difference we could make if we always encouraged others and spoke words that built others up. I am sure that what you do would soon be noticed and you would have opportunities to share the reason for your behavior.

* 2 Timothy 2:22

> Flee the evil desires of youth and pursue righteousness, faith, love and peace, along with those who call on the Lord out of a pure heart.

Paul was a realist even when talking to a keen follower of Jesus like Timothy. He knew that impure thoughts are normal and that Timothy would struggle with this issue as much as any human being. He urges Timothy to "flee" a word that shows how desperate the struggle is. This would include avoiding things that lead to impure thoughts.

For me that means avoiding many movies, television shows, women's magazines, and books. As the years go by, it means that there are more and more things I have to avoid as the world becomes more obviously impure.

As a teenager, I heard a sermon entitled, "Garbage in, garbage out." So simple, but a good life principle. If I want to be someone who honors Jesus then I must only fill my mind with things that please Him. 2 Timothy 2:22 reminds us that it is not good enough to simply stop doing something. We must also start doing something new; not just take off, but also put on.

* Philippians 4:8

Finally, brothers and sisters, whatever is true, whatever is noble, whatever is right, whatever is pure, whatever is lovely, whatever is admirable—if anything is excellent or praiseworthy—think about such things.

* Proverbs 15:26

The Lord detests the thoughts of the wicked, but those of the pure are pleasing to him.[1]

If we want to please God, then making purity a priority will delight Him. For it is the "pure in heart who will see God" (Matt. 5:8).

Most of this chapter has been about preventative measures. What if someone is already thoroughly enmeshed in impurity? What hope is there for them?

Hope for those already caught in impurity

King David's story can still be an encouragement. God loves you as much as He loved David and will make sure you are convicted of your sin. That is an important step to being restored to God. Once David realized his sin, he immediately perceived that his chief wrong was not against himself, Uriah or Bathsheba (although it was terrible for all of them, plus his entire family and nation) but against God Himself (2 Sam. 12:13). David's prayer of repentance in Psalm 51 is a treasure. Its words are a model of what we need to say to God. We must stop hiding (after all, how can we hide from a God who knows everything?) and admit that,

Against you, you only, have I sinned and done what is evil in your sight (Ps. 51:4).

Only after we have admitted our sin, can we then ask God for His forgiveness and cleansing. Amazingly, God has promised to hear these kinds of prayers and to remove our sins as "far as the east is from the west" (Ps. 103:12). If he could forgive King David, a liar, adulterer and murderer, then he can forgive you.

Sexual guilt is particularly tenacious. Satan loves to tell us that we're broken and the situation is irreparable. The good news of Jesus is that He can forgive, cleanse, and give us a new start. This does not mean that there will not be consequences in this life, but it does mean that there is hope.

Once God has dealt with our sin, then sword fighting (to deal with continued feelings of guilt) and having an accountability partner will be of immense help to prevent a repeat of the problem. God is more than powerful enough to help us become pure. Trust Him and keep using your sword whenever Satan tries to make you feel guilty and a failure (see previous chapters).

Reflection Questions:

1. What things are a danger to you in your struggle to stay pure?
2. What strategies in your life will help you to keep away from them?
3. Write down the ideas and verses from this chapter that you think will be most helpful. Add some of your own to them if necessary.
4. Find yourself an accountability partner whom you can trust. Choose someone who will be real and honest with you about their own sin and struggles.

Prayer Suggestions:

1. Read Psalm 51 and meditate on it. Turn its words into a prayer of repentance.
2. Praise God for His purity and holiness. Ask Him to help these things to characterize your life.

3. Ask God to provide an accountability partner for you in this area.

---

1. *New International Version* (Grand Rapids: Zondervan, 1984).

12

LOW SELF-ESTEEM

May was the sort of lady who was always overlooked. She was shy, quiet, and someone who blended in with the background. It was hard to have eye contact with her because she stooped.

I eventually noticed her because she was the most faithful attendee at my Bible studies. I was concerned about how she could ever be a pastor's wife, as her husband was studying at theological college. After praying about the situation, I approached her and asked if she would be willing to meet up with me once a week to study Ephesians.

May was someone whose thoughts ran on a circular track that told her, "You're hopeless, useless. How could anyone care or love you? How can you say you are a Christian? You're a failure and you can't even share your faith with others."

After explaining the sword fighting principles to May, we chose verses and principles for her to think about morning and evening.

The next week, I asked her how she had managed her sword practice and she sheepishly admitted that she had forgotten to do what I had asked. We went over the principles again. The next week she had again forgotten, despite not being a forgetful woman. I began to be suspicious. Was May experiencing some sort of direct spiritual opposition designed to prevent her dealing with her low self-esteem (see Chapter 14)? Satan doesn't fear someone who believes his lies or is self-absorbed, but he must be afraid of someone who looks at Jesus, begins to effectively wield their sword, and is transformed. We prayed particularly about her unusual forgetfulness and once again went over the principles.

A word of caution

Self-esteem is constantly talked about in Western society and in psychology. The opposite of low self-esteem is not high self-esteem but rather something I refer to as "God Esteem." That is, we are to see ourselves as God sees us.

Comparisons can skew our self-perceptions, as we compare ourselves either to some self-imposed standard or to other people. A standard we set for ourselves is a form of pride as we set ourselves up as the standard of judgement. Comparing ourselves to others is another twist on pride as we desire to make ourselves feel superior. What is desperately needed is for us to see reality, not some distorted false view.

Seeing ourselves as God sees us—the BAD news first

Over and over the gospel shows us a reality we want to deny and avoid, that we are totally rebellious against God. Adam and Eve's choice in the garden of Eden was not a slight misunderstanding or mistake. It wasn't an accident and couldn't be blamed on the snake, even though Eve tried to do so.

Their choice was a straight-out rebellion against a heavenly father who had given them everything including a perfect world to enjoy, perfect relationships, and responsibilities of caring for the world, and also friendship with God. They had never lacked a thing and God had not withheld anything good from them.

God's command was crystal clear.

You are free to eat from any tree in the garden; but you must not eat from the tree of the knowledge of good and evil, for when you eat from it you will certainly die (Gen. 2:17).

It cannot be clearer than that.

Were they really deceived by the snake or was that just a convenient blame-shifting excuse? They knew that God had only ever been generous to them but the snake played on their lack of contentment with what they had been given and tempted them to seek equality with God.

"You will not certainly die," the snake said. "For God knows that when you eat from it...you will *be like God*" (Gen. 3:7, emphasis added).

Their choice was a deliberate rebellion because they had been warned of the consequences.

Adam and Eve chose to believe a complete stranger over God.

The Bible goes on to drive the bad news home. The sheer bluntness of the message can make us cringe and protest.

For example, "You were dead in your...sins" (Eph. 2:1). We are born dead; walking corpses, unable to do anything to bring life to ourselves. That is offensive in any culture. No wonder we don't want to believe it. We are so proud that we prefer to think that we either have a "good heart" or a mere "sickness." We want to be able to pridefully say that "we're not too bad" and deserve salvation.

But in Jeremiah 17:9, we're told that,

The heart is deceitful above all things and beyond cure.

Why does religiosity thrive on people striving to be good? Because we refuse to believe the truth that "we are beyond cure."

Romans 3:10–12 is like a hammer striking an anvil (read this slowly, aloud, emphasis added).

There is *no one* righteous, *not even one...No one* who seeks God...*All* have turned away...

It is tempting to skip over these realities, but we must not. If we don't see the dreadfulness of our sin and the magnitude of our problem, we will never grasp the breadth of God's love demonstrated on the cross. Instead, we will be filled with pride and self-justification, and will disregard the huge cost of the cross, minimizing and reducing it to less that it really is.

The dazzling reality of the cross can only be appreciated against the inky black backdrop of our sin problem. As Tim Keller has said, "The gospel is this: We are more sinful and flawed in ourselves than we ever dared believe, yet at the very same time we are more loved and accepted in Jesus Christ than we ever dared hope."[1]

Here are some of the Bible verses and principles that we chose for May. You might come up with others that have particular meaning for you.

How does God view me?

* Genesis 1:26 says that we are made in the image of God. God gave us His very best, so He must think we are special.

* Psalm 139:1–23, 13–14, 16

You have searched me, Lord, and you know me. You know when I sit...rise...you are familiar with all my ways...knit me together in my mother's womb...Fearfully and wonderfully made...All the days ordained for me were written in your book before one of them came to be.

This psalm contains enough truths to meditate on for weeks. If God "knit us together in our mother's womb," then he made us in a certain way for a certain purpose. This is true no matter what the world thinks about us. Even our disability can be used by God to bring Him glory.[2]

Our personality, our weaknesses and strengths, if they are turned over to God, can be used for His purposes, and that includes bringing Him glory. Our combination of characteristics means that we can share Jesus in certain unique ways with certain kinds of people. That is awe-inspiring.

* Ephesians 1:4

[God] Chose us in him before the creation of the world.

It is no coincidence that we are Christians. For some reason God chose us to follow Him. It was not because we were more beautiful or smarter or more worthy than anyone else (Deut. 7:7ff., 9:4ff.) but simply because of His grace. He does nothing by accident but has a purpose in everything. Think about what it means that we were chosen before the creation of the world. It was no whim of God's or a sudden change in plan. Before the creation of the world He knew who you would be and His purposes for you. If that doesn't create a sense of in you, nothing will!

* Ephesians 1:5

In love, he predestined us for adoption to sonship.

This is not to exclude women but is stronger than simply saying we are adopted as daughters. For in those days, daughters had few rights. To be adopted as sons means much more than simply becoming God's children, for we are to be the ones that inherit the rights of sons.

Think about what it means to be adopted as sons of the King of the universe. I have always thought that to be adopted is far more special than to be a biological child. After all, the parent doesn't choose the child who is born to them and must simply parent the one they receive. But it is clear God wants us and chooses to elevate us to be His children.

A famous photo was taken in the 1960s of the then American President, John F. Kennedy, sitting at his official desk in the White

House. Under the desk and at his feet, his infant son happily played. President Kennedy represented all the authority of a superpower at work, but his son knew nothing of this. To him, the President was his daddy. John Junior had direct and daily access to the President of the United States. As children of God, we have direct access to the King of kings.

* Ephesians 2:10

> For we are God's handiwork, created in Christ Jesus to do good works, which God prepared in advance for us to do.

The word "handiwork" suggests care and creativity. We are like a piece of exquisite jewelry, or a reconditioned vintage car from the 1920s. Every care and much love has gone into creating us. Meditating on this word should make us sit in awe at God's feet. How can we dare to claim that something God made is not good? This verse also speaks to us regardless of our appearance or abilities, or our perceived lack of them. God has a plan and purpose in the way we are made. Each of us is unique and special. The verse goes on to tell us that we were not just made to be looked at but to be useful. The 1920s Packard car might be beautiful but real pleasure comes when you drive it and use it for its purpose. God has prepared good works for each of us to do. He has made us each to do unique tasks that bring Him glory. Ask Him to show you what they are.

* 1 Corinthians 1:27–29

> God chose the foolish things of the world to shame the wise; God chose the weak things of the world to shame the strong. God chose the lowly things of this world and the despised things—and the things that are not—to nullify the things that are, so that no one may boast before him.

These verses have had a profound impact on my life. When Satan tells me I am weak and useless, I laugh and say, "How right you are!

Praise God I am, because when people see me do things that are beyond my abilities, then they will know that they are only possible because of what God has done in my life."

The weaker we are the better, at least from God's point of view.

* Think about the fact that God loved us so much that He came to die for us (even when we tell Him that we don't need Him and His death means nothing to us).

Thinking about what God has done in dying for me, makes me feel special and overwhelmingly grateful.

* Any number of other verses may help you. Make your own list, but don't forget to reflect first on your desperate sin and the contrast of God's marvelous love.

And what about May? She came back the following week and it was evident that she was beginning to see herself in a completely different way. Constant repetition of God's word and reminding herself how God viewed her brought her a new appreciation of God's greatness, purposes, and grace. She responded in thanksgiving and praise to God. Within a few months, she had the confidence to apply the sword of the Spirit in other areas of her life and started sharing about Jesus at work. Even her posture changed as she straightened up and started to glow, confident in God's love. Two of her friends quickly noticed the difference and wanted to know her Savior too.

Reflection Questions:

1. What particular attacks does Satan make on you in this area?
2. What is the difference between "self" esteem and "God" esteem?
3. Compile your own list of references to fight this issue.
4. How could you share this truth with a non-Christian?

Prayer Suggestions:

1. Praise God for who He has made you to be.

2. Pray asking God to help you believe that you are loved.

---

1. Timothy Keller and Kathy Keller, *The Meaning of Marriage: Facing the Complexities of Commitment with the Wisdom of God* (New York: Penguin Random House, 2013), 48.
2. Reading of any of Joni Eareckson Tada's books or articles will be helpful. https://www.joniandfriends.org

13
DISCOURAGEMENT AND DEPRESSION

This is the chapter I have found most difficult to write. Mostly because there is still much debate about the causes of depression and its treatment. Depression is neither simple to understand nor easy to treat. It is a multi-faceted condition.

Depression has been defined as a "Psychiatric disorder showing symptoms such as *persistent* feelings of hopelessness, dejection, poor concentration, lack of energy, inability to sleep, and sometimes suicidal tendencies."[1]

The causes of depression can include a response to traumatic or stressful life events (reactive depression) or chemical and hormonal imbalances in our bodies. Genetic factors also seem to play a part. Depression is strongly associated with poor sleep and being generally run-down and exhausted physically, emotionally, and spiritually.

For those who are depressed, it might encourage you to know you're not alone. Some of the world's spiritual greats have suffered depression either occasionally or repeatedly: David Brainerd (missionary); C. H. Spurgeon (preacher and pastor); J. B. Phillips (Bible translator); Hudson Taylor (founder of the China Inland Mission, now known as OMF) and such Biblical heroes as Elijah, Job, and Jeremiah. They too felt as if they were walking under a dark cloud of despair and purposelessness.

After university, I worked as a physiotherapist in several different hospitals. I saw many people struggling to cope following major health challenges: stroke, spinal injury, and especially health challenges impacting body image like mastectomy or amputation. It is particularly difficult to adjust to circumstances that may not improve. This kind of depression would seem to be normal. Wouldn't anyone struggle with these issues?

The treatment of depression is usually multidisciplinary. This book does not aim to deal with the medical side but only the issue of sword fighting. Please don't assume that medical treatment is not necessary. In some of the situations described in this chapter, the people were suicidal. Each of them also needed medical help before they were able to begin using the sword. Medication brought them a measure of stability so that they could begin to manage their uncontrollable thoughts.

Biblical examples

Job went through more loss in a short period of time than most of us will ever go through. His eventual depression was reactive, that is, his depression was set off by a series of major losses. In his case, the death of all his children in a single roof collapse (three daughters and seven sons), the loss of nearly all his economic stability (flocks of camels, goats, and donkeys) and then physical pain (boils) and the loss of health (Job 1). To make matters worse, his wife came to him and said, "Are you still maintaining your integrity? Curse God and die" (Job 2:9).

Job seems to have understood how to sword fight because he consistently spoke God's truth into the situation and did not slip into depression. But then his friends turned up and started hammering at him with all sorts of falsehoods along the lines of, "You must have sinned because otherwise you wouldn't be suffering." Even then, Job remained strong, but it was God's silence that eventually wore him down. Eventually he cried out,

> Why is life given to a man whose way is hidden, whom God has hedged in? For sighing has become my daily food; my groans pour out like water. What I feared has come upon me; what I dreaded has happened to me. I have no peace, no quietness; I have no rest, but only turmoil (Job 3:23–26).

A sleepless Job suffered from a sense of abandonment both by his family and friends and ultimately, by God.

Abandonment and the subsequent isolation are common factors in depression. Welch's article in the *Journal of Biblical Counselling* is rather dated but is in fact very helpful. He says,

> The experience of depression is that nobody is present. They feel like they are in a hermetically sealed bubble that keeps them from real contact with other people...their feelings deny the promises of God...They say that God is far away and doesn't hear. Most depressed people don't realize that although their feelings might say something that is very important, feelings can also lie.[2]

Welch makes the interesting observation that in community-based cultures there is a much lower rate of depression.[3] This suggests that one of the things that helps is that both friends and family work hard at ensuring the depressed person is not left alone and therefore does not feel isolated. The person with depression often feels too exhausted to relate to people. Friends can come alongside and work to build a small but supportive community around the depressed person.

Many people have observed that the best thing Job's friends did was to sit with him for seven days without saying anything. It was when they tried to sort things out and bring meaning to his suffering, that they added to his pain.

Scriptures for those feeling isolated

Meditating on God's Word is essential because if Satan can convince us we are alone and that no one understands our situation, then it is easy for him to win the battle. The following are just a tiny selection of the many verses and stories that might help us combat this Satanic lie.

* Hebrews 13:5b

Never will I leave you; never will I forsake you.

* Joshua 1:9b

Be strong and courageous. Do not be afraid; do not be discouraged, for the Lord your God will be with you wherever you go.

There are many other verses that remind us that even if we feel isolated, or are isolated, that God is *always* with us. He will never abandon us. We must choose to believe this and trust these promises.

* Stories

There are many stories of people in the Bible who felt alone, discouraged, and fearful. As well as Joshua and Elijah there was Moses (Exod. 3ff.) and Gideon (Judg. 6ff.).

During our lives, many of us might have bouts of reactive discouragement which could slide towards depression. We can't avoid losses. Such losses could be linked with miscarriage or barrenness, singleness, domestic violence, a bad marriage or divorce, the death of family members or friends, chronic pain or health issues, unemployment, just to name a few. The degree of impact is related to a complex web of gender, personality, expectations, the closeness of relationship and the particular nature of a relationship. The degree of loss we feel may not be logical. For example, we might grieve more for someone we have been estranged from than for someone we have been close to. All these losses are also filtered through a web of our own beliefs, values, past history, and past hurts.

Job isn't the only Biblical character we can learn from. In contrast to Job, Elijah's depression had different causes. For years, despite threats to his life, Elijah seemed to be holding things together. Outwardly, he coped well while living in hiding from King Ahab in a remote valley. His exile included three years of being fed by ravens (1 Kings 17:2–6) and a Sidonian woman (vv. 7–24). Isolation was definitely an issue for him. He did not have anybody of his own age or culture nearby and in addition, Elijah believed he was the only one left faithful to God. This belief, which we later learn is false, compounds Elijah's sense of isolation.

God then sends Elijah to Mount Carmel where Elijah confronts the prophets of Baal. Here Elijah sees God do the amazing miracles of sending fire from heaven and also ending the three-year drought. It is following this climax that Elijah comes crashing down and he gives way to fear and finally sinks so low that he begs God to let him die (1 Kings 19:3–4). For sometimes discouragement and depression come after times of intense victory and spiritual highs.

There are strong hints that Elijah was run-down physically because it was at this stage God allowed him to have two long periods of sleep. God also provided food for him through an angel and sent him on a long journey. God never rebuked Elijah in any way we might expect. Instead He met with Elijah and recommissioned him. God also showed Elijah that he was mistaken in thinking he alone was being faithful to God when He said,

> Yet I reserve seven thousand in Israel—all whose knees have not bowed down to Baal and whose mouths have not kissed him (1 Kings 19:18).

Practical considerations

Dealing with depression requires us to be persistent for the long haul. Welch writes that,

> Satan wages spiritual attacks with...suggestions that God does not really love or care, that he is indifferent to our pain, perhaps even sadistic, or that God doesn't even exist. This must be countered with steady volleys of the love of Christ, directed at the depressed person's heart.[4]

We need to spend time with those suffering depression and be a real friend who doesn't just accept what they say as truth, but who refutes it and points them continually to Jesus and the truths found in Scripture.[5] This will not only be good for them but for us too.

Scriptures to remind us of God's love
*Romans 8:35, 37ff.

> Who shall separate us from the love of Christ? Shall trouble or hardship or persecution or famine or nakedness or danger or sword?...No, in all these things we are more than conquerors through him who loved us. For I am convinced that neither death nor life, neither angels nor demons, neither the present nor the future, nor any powers, neither height nor depth, nor anything else in all creation, will be able to separate us from the love of God that is in Christ Jesus our Lord.

No matter how we feel, these verses remind us that it is impossible for God to let us go. He is with us in life and death and even through the depths of depression. Memorize this promise, recite it often, and eventually this truth will go from being mere head knowledge to heart knowledge.

*The cross of Christ

We must soak ourselves in the story of the cross, the story of the God who dies for His enemies and those who denied and mocked and betrayed Him. As Romans 5:8 says,

But God demonstrates his own love for us in this: While we were still sinners, Christ died for us.

Welch reminds us that depression is a wonderful opportunity to deal with issues that will be brought to the surface.[6] We are mistaken if we say that depression is the result of sin or a punishment from God (like Job's friends), but it is useful to ask what it is that the depressed person fears, or is guilty, angry, or in despair about. This will highlight issues that need to be exposed to the light of the gospel and dealt with according to the principles of God's word. Sometimes depression is a response that helps us avoid dealing with issues, like for my friend who was terrified of death.

Too often in depression, a person is listening to a broken record of Satan's lies and believing them. Such people need to say to themselves, "You have been listening to your own thoughts, but now you must begin to listen to what God says in His word and to what God says through other people."[7]

As a friend who comes alongside a depressed person, Welch says,

> We do not just enter their world, we want to call them out...depression...[skews] almost every interpretation. As a result, those who are depressed, need to leave their dark interpretations behind and enter into the radical, sometimes upside-down perspectives that God gives in Scripture.[8]
>
> In depression, the new way of living is to believe and act on what God says rather than to feel what God says. It is living by faith...In other words, when there is a debate between what your feelings say and what Scripture says, Scripture must be allowed to win. If there is any other result then you are essentially telling God that He is not to be trusted.[9]

One lady I discipled was especially difficult to work with. She had severe depression and could only concentrate for no more than thirty minutes at a time.

Initially, she was frustrated with me because I didn't want to spend extremely long periods of time listening to her thoughts. Her thoughts were suicidal and she was constantly listening to and believing Satan's lies about her feelings of uselessness. Her depression was so severe that each time we spoke I could only share with her about one paragraph of Scripture and then pray.

We slowly went through some sections of Luke and she was surprised how relevant each section was. I asked her to repeat one truth from the passage to herself until we met again and I also taught her about thanksgiving (see later section). Over the following eight weeks, she saw steady progress as she slowly came to believe what Jesus said.

Once she moved away, several friends continued to love her and remind her of God's truths. Two years later, she was a very different person and had begun to learn the hard lesson of making the right life choices. Choices to not allow herself to become too busy and run-down, either physically or emotionally.

Jill was someone I discipled in Taiwan. Her depression was so severe that she planned to kill her children and then commit suicide. She used alcohol and drugs to numb her pain. Not surprisingly, her thoughts of suicide were strongest when she was drunk.

Thankfully, a friend took her to a doctor. This man was not only a good doctor, but a Christian who recognized that depression can also be a spiritual issue. He pointed Jill towards Jesus. It turned out that God had already been working in Jill's life. She'd started reading the Bible on her own and soon discerned that the cult group she was attending did not truly know Jesus. The doctor introduced her to true followers of Jesus and Jill quickly found the God she had been searching for.

I had the privilege of meeting up with Jill every week and we studied the Bible together, as we worked on sword practice. Within a few months she was well on the way to "taking every thought captive" and "being transformed by the renewing of [her] mind" (Rom. 12:2).

Jill is still prone to depression. She knows that if she becomes overtired and doesn't do regular exercise, then she is more likely to believe Satan's lies, so she works hard at maintaining a healthy lifestyle. She can recognize Satan's lies and is seldom depressed for long because she is spiritually fit.

Jill is now full of joy. This is despite all she has suffered, and continues to suffer, for being a Christian through beatings, emotional pressure, threats and constant ridicule. Against all the lies that have been thrown at her, she uses her sword and allows the Bible to show her how God views each situation.

Early stages of depression

As with many kinds of sickness, prevention is easier than cure. If a Christian is experienced in sword fighting, they may not even slide into depression.

I once worked on a church planting team. Three of the team had a history of depression that had required medication. Over a six-month period, we were all discouraged from lack of results in our evangelism and were also struggling with poor sleep and the resultant exhaustion. Our minds were full of thoughts like, "You're working hard but what is being achieved?" or "How can you justify the money that is being spent on you?" or "Perhaps you're not suited to this job." or "Why not go back to your home and be successful?" Considering how little sleep I was getting (sometimes waking 30–40 times a night for two years), these thoughts had a wonderful kind of logic. However, I was blessed to have already had quite a bit of sword practice.

As a team we discussed passages and principles of Scripture to combat our feelings of discouragement:

* The results of evangelism are God's responsibility (1 Cor. 3:5–7). Our responsibility was to continue in prayer, sharing wisely and gently (Col. 4:2–6; 1 Pet. 3:15–16) and to leave the results to God.

* 1 Corinthians 4:2

Now it is required that those who have been given a trust must prove faithful.

God requires faithfulness, not human measures of success, for being faithful is success in His eyes.

* We reviewed Satan's purposes (e.g. John 8:44; 1 Pet. 5:8) and his methods and were able to discern his part in what was happening to us. After all, how often do three out of four co-workers in gospel ministry all struggle with depression at the same time? Just recognizing that we were under spiritual attack meant we were more alert.

In addition, we all discussed why we might have been feeling depressed and all agreed that there were some precipitating factors (tiredness, and a poor work and rest balance). We all worked hard at having a weekly day off and discussed what that needed to be (good sleep and rest, rather than a day to catch up on email or other tasks) as well as making sure we had at least three exercise sessions a week. We kept each other accountable for these things and regularly prayed about them for each member of the leadership team.

We also recruited all our prayer partners to pray and we spent more time praying ourselves. In the following three years, we were alert for the first signs of spiritual attack and immediately started our sword fighting, and other strategies, whenever they were needed. Subsequently, none of the team required medical intervention.

Reactive depression

Also known as "situational depression," reactive depression "can develop after you experience a traumatic event or series of events…a type of adjustment disorder."[10]

In dealing with this type of depression, firstly, we need to focus on the sovereign control of God, who is all-powerful and never surprised by an event or too busy to care.

Helpful Bible verses might include:

* Jeremiah 32:17, 19

> Sovereign Lord, you have made the heavens and the earth by your great power...nothing is too hard for you...great are your purposes and mighty are your deeds.

In response to this verse, spend time meditating on creation and how it reflects the greatness of God and His attention to detail. If God is able to create the world, then He is able to help us with our depression and its cause. He can heal or He can give us the ability to cope with it.

It would be worthwhile thinking through the stories of people in the Bible who have had to deal with an issue similar to ours and seeing how God helped them and what they learnt through their pain. Think of Joseph, dealing with rejection by family and false accusations of wrongdoing (Gen. 37–50), or Elijah, fleeing for his life (1 Kings 19), or Peter dealing with failure after he denied Jesus three times (Luke 23:54ff.), or Hannah with childlessness (1 Sam. 1).

* Romans 8:28–29

> We know that in all things God works for the good of those who have been called according to his purpose [and this purpose is]...to be conformed to the image of his Son.

This is not a promise that everything will be magically cured. Instead, it is a promise that if we trust God, He will use everything, including our failures and sufferings, to make us more like Jesus. It might be that God's plan is for us to become or remain a widow, or be single, or die of cancer, but He promises that no problem is too big for Him to achieve His purpose of making us like Jesus.

My favorite pastoral visits are those when I meet a mature believer facing death. When someone has really grasped God's truths, then these visits are full of joy. We may weep together but they are tears of grief mixed with an indescribable joy.

* It is also important to remind ourselves why bad things happen. They often happen to good people and we want to cry, "It's so unfair." If we get stuck on that cry, then we will spiral down into complaints, anger against God, and possibly depression.

We need to preach the gospel to ourselves again. Firstly, we need to go back to Genesis 3 and realize that the pain in the world came about because people rejected God as King. Sadly, we too want to run our own lives. The pain of sickness, death, failure, and injustice is the end result. We need to remind ourselves of how far God went to remedy the situation and save us. Philippians 2 describes the distance that God came to rescue us; from the glory and perfection of heaven to the humiliation and suffering of earth.

* Well-meaning people often transmit the lies of Satan as they visit. When my aunt was dying of cancer at thirty-four, she had many visitors who told her that the reason she had cancer was that she had sinned. She was also told that she needed to repent and have faith and then she would be healed. God specifically refutes that idea several times in the Bible (Luke 13:1–5; John 9:1–2).

In Job's case, his four friends all believed that Job must have sinned for him to be suffering as he was. Their comfort sent Job towards despair. For Job was never given the reason for his suffering. We, as the readers, are privileged to have been told that there was a bigger issue behind his story—a divine battle between God and Satan. Satan declared that God was not innately worthy of praise, that people only loved and praised God because of the gifts that God gave them. Satan's challenge was for God to take everything away from Job and then Job would demonstrate that God was not worthy of praise apart from the gifts He gave. It was a huge contest that God won because His weak and depressed servant, Job, still trusted God even in his pain and confusion.

Have you ever wondered why Job is never told the story of the divine competition? I have. God does something different than I would have done (indeed He usually does!) God asks Job a series of questions designed to show Job that there is a lot that he doesn't understand. God is asking in effect, "if you can't even create and look after an animal, then who are you to question me? Be content and trust me." Job gets the point and chooses to trust God even when he has received no explanation of his suffering.

Jesus' disciples also had the same point of view as Job's comforters. It is a point of view that Hindus and Buddhists would agree with, as it is the law of cause and effect (Karma). If you are good, then you'll be blessed and if you're bad, you'll be cursed. The disciples revealed that this was their thinking in Luke 13:1–5 and John 9. When they met a man born blind, or heard that people had died in a tower collapse, they assumed it must be because that person or their parents had sinned.

Jesus gives two insights. In the case of the blind man, he says that he was allowed to be blind all those years so that "the works of God might be displayed in him" (John 9:3). We might argue, "but why did he have to suffer for so many years?" Instead we are asked to trust that God's timing is right and that He achieves the most glory (people coming to trust Him and praise Him) through this healing at this time.

The second insight is in Luke 13. Jesus warns the disciples that there are worse outcomes than dying or suffering: it would be infinitely worse to die and go to hell than to suffer while on this earth. Thus, one purpose of suffering is to be a warning light which forces us to think about eternal issues and to repent now before it is too late. I have certainly found this to be true. Many of my friends have come to Christ because they have gone through suffering. When life is smooth, they don't need to think about God. However, when life falls apart, they are forced to confront issues they have avoided and God is graciously waiting for them.

*A final encouragement comes from the life of Jesus. He is the only one whom we can know for certain never sinned, and yet he went through the greatest suffering. At the very least, He experienced the death of His earthly father (otherwise there would be no need for Jesus while on the Cross to appoint John to look after his mother—John 20:26–27); He bore the stigma of being thought illegitimate (few would have believed Mary's story of a virgin birth); He was misunderstood by all His family (Luke 2:50; John 7:3–5); He was opposed and ridiculed by religious leaders and crowds (John 7:20, 30–52); He was betrayed by one of His closest friends (Luke 20:1–6, 22:48) and denied by another (Peter in Luke 22:54–62).

All this does not include the normal sufferings of living on this earth (sickness, failure, disappointment) and then the final pain of unjust accusation, beating and crucifixion, to say nothing of separation from heaven and all its joys. This demonstrates once and for all that there is not a direct cause and effect relationship between sin and suffering for sometimes, the totally innocent suffer.

Denial, questioning, disappointment, and anger are normal stages of grief. The problem comes when we get stuck and do not refute Satan's lie that a certain stage is permanent with our sword of the Spirit. We are not to wallow in self-pity and anger that leads only to increased depression. Instead, we are called to trust God and to continue to take every thought captive. When we fail to do this, we need to come humbly to the Lord, repent, and ask His forgiveness. At that point, Satan will try to make us doubt that God can forgive and we must once again pick up our sword and refute his lies.

* 1 John 1:9

> If we confess our sins, he is faithful and just and will forgive us our sins and purify us from all unrighteousness.

* Psalm 103:12

> As far as the east is from the west, so far has he removed our transgressions from us.

Both of these verses need to be believed and memorized so that every time that Satan whispers, "God can't or won't forgive that," we are able to recite them and counter his lies.

Thanksgiving—a practical tip

One of the difficulties we face in depression is wallowing in negativity. It is all too easy to become a complainer. A major part of the solution for complaining is to do the opposite so we must actively practice thanksgiving.

Donna, a lady I discipled, lived a really tough life. Her twenty-year-old son had died in a car accident. In response, her husband became an alcoholic and not surprisingly, the younger son didn't want to come home too often.

When I suggested thanksgiving to Donna, she said, "I don't have anything to be thankful for!"

I started by asking her if she had eaten anything delicious that day? Yes, she had, so I suggested we start by thanking God for that. Then we moved on to pleasant things she had heard or seen. As we kept going, starting from the most mundane, she realized that she actually had a lot of things to thank God for. We then started on all the things found in the Bible that were linked with our salvation and the facts of God creating and choosing us. That kept us going for another ten minutes.

I then suggested that she write a list of all these things and pray through it, morning and evening. Within a few days, she was amazed at how grateful to God she had become. Her situation might never change but her attitude was changing. Instead of constantly complaining and being miserable, she was well on the way to being joyful.[11]

When God commands us to "rejoice always" (Phil. 4:4) He has a reason for it. We are not to be people who deny reality, but we are to be people who rejoice in God and praise and thank Him, no matter our circumstances.

J. O. Fraser was a CIM missionary in Yunnan with the Lisu people. These words are recorded in his biography, *Mountain Rain*.[12]

> He was assailed by deep and treacherous doubts. Hath God said? The question came to him again and again, as clearly as it came at the dawn of time. Your prayers are not being answered, are they? No one wants to hear your message. The few who first believed

have gone back, haven't they? You see, it doesn't work. You should have never stayed in this area on such a fool's errand. You've been in China five years and there's not much to show for it, is there? You thought you were called to be a missionary; it was pure imagination. You'd better leave it all, go back and admit it was a big mistake.

Day after day and night after night he wrestled with doubt and suicidal despair. Suicidal? Not once, but several times he stared over the dark ravine into the abyss. Why not end it all?

James then received a letter that contained a copy of a magazine. In it was an article talking about using Scripture to resist Satan. He writes,

> I found that it worked! That cloud of depression dispersed. I found that I could have victory in the spiritual realm whenever I wanted it…The victory was, of course, a spiritual one. The outward circumstances were the same as before.

Later, as he grew in his experience to use his sword he wrote,

> Formerly it used to take me days to recover from such defeat (depression). Then…it took a few hours. Now I know even that to be too long, and only allow a few minutes for complete recovery.[13]

Could depression ever be useful?
Again Welch writes,

> We are under the mistaken impression that divine love cannot coexist with human pain. This is one of Satan's most effective strategies and it must be attacked with the gospel of grace.[14]

We must be messengers of hope to anyone who is depressed. By looking at Biblical examples, and even in the lives of other Christians, we need to remind our friend (and ourselves) that God never wastes anything that we submit to Him and God only ever wants our best. That best is not our happiness and ease (this is certainly a lie from the world!) but our maturity (Rom. 8:28–29). God can even use going through depression to mature us. What is even more amazing is that if we submit to Jesus, He can take our experiences to be used in ministry. As 2 Corinthians 1:3–4 says, "Praise be to the God and Father of our Lord Jesus Christ, the Father of compassion and the God of all comfort, who comforts us in all our troubles, so that we can comfort those in any trouble with the comfort we ourselves receive from God."

Those who have walked through the valley of depression can say to others, "I have been there, I understand and there is hope. Let me share how Jesus helped me."

Any child of God who has struggled with an issue (depression included) and seen Jesus use it to bring about their maturity, becomes more understanding, compassionate and ultimately useful as a minister in God's expanding kingdom.

Reflection Questions:

1. Have you suffered any sort of discouragement or depression? What verses or principles could have helped you?

2. Create your own list of verses or principles and start applying them in your life.

3. On a scale of 0–10, how thankful are you?

4. What are the results of not being thankful? Of being thankful?

5. How could you become more thankful?

Prayer Suggestions:

1. Practice praying and being thankful.

1. Macintosh computer internal dictionary but similar definitions can be found on WHO sites and mental health sites online.
2. E. T. Welch, "Understanding Depression," *Journal of Biblical Counseling* 18, no. 2 (Winter 2000): 9–10.
3. Welch, "Understanding Depression," 16–19.
4. Welch, "Understanding Depression," 14.
5. Welch, "Understanding Depression," 10.
6. Welch, "Understanding Depression," 10.
7. E. T. Welch, "Words of Hope for Those Who Struggle with Depression," *Journal of Biblical Counseling* 18, no. 2 (Winter 2000): 41.
8. Welch, "Words of Hope," 27.
9. Welch, "Words of Hope," 41.
10. https://www.healthline.com/health/depression/situational-depression
11. The Bible also eventually leads us to the perspective that even things that don't feel "good" can be for our good (Heb. 12:5–11) . Philippians 4:4 tells us to rejoice always and presumably this includes rejoicing over things that don't feel good at all.
12. Eileen Crossman, *Mountain Rain* (Carlisle: Authentic Media, 1982), 71–72.
13. Crossman, *Mountain Rain*, 119.
14. Welch, "Understanding Depression," 14.

14
DIRECT SPIRITUAL ATTACK

At the end of two years of full-time language study, I started work in a Taiwanese church and was heavily involved in evangelism and discipleship. One night as I slept, I felt a man's hands around my neck strangling me. At the same time, I experienced paralyzing fear and saw myself standing on the brink of hell and noxious vapors of fear were blowing up towards me. I knew immediately that this was a direct demonic attack and called out, "Jesus, help," and the hands and fear were gone.

This was a new experience for me. I had never heard of such experiences in the Western context. Full of trepidation about what the other missionaries would think of me, I shared my nightmare with a more senior colleague and was relieved to discover that this experience was quite common among missionaries.

Since then, I have heard a multitude of such stories, from other missionaries (both short- and long-term), from locals, and increasingly from those in Western countries too.

All the experiences have some things in common:

- The dreams are extremely vivid, very different to ordinary

nightmares, as the person is self-aware and able to think and speak in the dream and often finds it difficult to discern whether they are awake or asleep.
- Strangling or difficulty breathing is common. People often describe a heavy pressure on their chest.
- The person also clearly remembers the dream in the morning.[1]

After I had experienced several of these dreams, I began to mention them more often and discovered that many people in Asia (locals and missionaries) had similar experiences. In the case of locals, the nightmares were often around the time they were making a decision about whether or not to follow Jesus. Through the dreams, they came under considerable pressure to reject Jesus.

Since my first home assignment, I have shared my experiences as part of a board game where participants experience the disappointments and joys of missionary life. If they rolled a "6" on the dice, I would say, "You've lost a turn, because you've come under direct spiritual attack."

On my earlier home assignments, these stories seemed to surprise the listeners and so I would explain what I meant by the term, "spiritual attack" and share several testimonies. However, on subsequent home assignments, it has become more common for participants to say they have had similar experiences.

It is important that we discern between ordinary nightmares and demonic ones. The points mentioned previously help, but it is also helpful to ask what the dreams aim to achieve. They usually come at times of important spiritual ministry. For example, before an important series of talks, meetings or outreach; or times when people are seriously making disciples or about to train others in evangelism, discipleship and church planting.

One particularly underhanded way the enemy uses is to attack adults through their children.

My parents were also missionaries and when I was a young

toddler, there was a period of time when I would sleepwalk and say in a horrible, flat voice, "Bong, bong, I hate Jesus. Bong, bong, I hate Jesus."

This greatly distressed them as they had never encountered such a situation before. There were no books or Internet to look up about such a situation and they were too embarrassed to talk to other missionaries, in case the organization sent them home or concluded they were poor parents.

Eventually, they spoke to another more experienced worker who told them about some of the ways Satan attacks and urged them to gather some prayer warriors and to pray for my protection before bed each night.

The problem was resolved and they were also able to work out why I said "Bong, bong." From my room, I was able to hear the gong in a local temple as it was struck to put people into a trance ready for demon possession.

Was I possessed then? My parents never cast a demon out of me but I was certainly oppressed externally and was being used to cause my parents distress. However, once they recognized what was happening, they were able to put a wall of protective prayer around me.

I have heard of several such stories, including a child who used to say to their parents as they went out the door to a ministry opportunity, "Please don't tell anyone about Jesus or I will have terrible nightmares."

Sadly, for quite some time, the parents listened to the child's words and didn't seek help, probably for the same reasons as my parents. Our enemy is talented at isolating us and convincing us that we are the only ones who suffer through a situation. His aim is to silence the good news and make us useless for God's Kingdom. If we do feel useless enough, it is easy for us to simply give up and remain silent. However, if we have the courage to open our mouths and share our stresses and weaknesses, we almost always discover that we're not alone and that others are able to discern what is going on.

SWORD FIGHTING

There is no magic formula to rebuking Satan in such a dream attack. What is important is to call out to Jesus and to trust him. Many people say something about their position in Christ, for instance, "I am a child of the King of the Universe. You have no power over me. In the name of Jesus, leave me alone."

These frontal attacks make it much easier to understand what the enemy is up to. If we don't stand on the promises of God and use scriptural truths to refute Satan, then we will be bound in fear. Once we give in to fear, then Satan seems to gain a foothold for further influence in our lives.

The following are some verses and stories that might be helpful:

* 1 John 4:4

> ...the one who is in you is greater than the one who is in the world.

We must never imagine that Satan's power in any way equals God's. They are in no way "equal but opposite." God's power is far, far superior to anything Satan has to offer.

* Mark 1:21–28

This is just one of many possible demonstrations of Jesus' power over Satan and his demons (Mark 5:1ff.; Luke 4:31ff.). The people were amazed that Jesus could simply say, "Be quiet!" and command the demon to leave. All these stories are demonstrations of the truth found in 1 John 4:4.

* Some of the verses on fear from previous chapters and remind us that God is with us (Josh. 1:9; Heb. 5:13).

* Romans 8:31b, 38, 39

> If God is for us, who can be against us?...I am convinced that neither death nor life, *neither angels nor demons*, neither the present nor the future, nor any powers, neither height nor depth, nor anything else in all creation, will be able to separate us from the love of God that is in Christ Jesus our Lord (emphasis added).

Our enemy will try to convince us that God is far away or can't save us. These verses remind us that any such claim is a lie.

———

During a time when I was heavily involved in evangelism, I had three days of terrible headaches. I battled on assuming that these headaches were just extreme examples of the headaches that I get which are linked to my upper neck. Suddenly the thought flashed into my mind that the headaches weren't normal but supernatural. I always hesitate to assume something is supernatural, but I spoke into the room and said something like, "Satan if these headaches are from you, I want you to know that nothing will ever stop me sharing the good news of Jesus with others. I am His child and you have no hold over me. In Jesus' name leave me alone." Immediately the headaches were gone and I have never had such headaches again.

Satan seems to have temporarily given up on this kind of direct attack in my life, perhaps because I so quickly identified the attack as from Satan and applied Scripture to it. Instead, I suspect that he is now using more subtle approaches because they are more difficult to discern. These could include a flurry of distractions or an outbreak of relationship difficulties that are emotionally draining. As long as we fail to discern such devious approaches, we are unlikely to realize we're under spiritual attack and so we won't wield our sword.

Reflection Questions:

1. What do you believe about Satan's methods? Justify them from Scripture.

2. How can we avoid blaming everything on Satan and shirking the responsibility for our own sin? There are groups who think that all sin and weakness is caused by demonic possession. Their "healing" methods major on casting out the demons. How could you discern what is true?

3. Why might there be far less discussion or even knowledge of this issue in Western contexts? If possible, go and question some non-Westerners to discover their experiences in this area. Don't try to impose your views. Rather listen and then compare their experiences with the Bible.

4. Can you see any situations in your life that might have been Satanic attacks? How could you avoid giving Satan too much credit?

5. How has this chapter changed your views?

6. How would you deal (from Scripture) with such an attack? It is worth thinking about this before an attack comes.

Prayer Suggestions:

1. Praise God for who He is and His power over Satan and his demons.

2. Ask God for His protection over you and your family and ministry.

---

1. Another missionary says that she was not asleep when she saw these "nightmares." They were more like visions.

15
BITTERNESS AND RESENTMENT

There are some people who might be tempted to think, "Yes, the Bible is useful for all the issues you have mentioned previously, but surely it can't be useful in my situation where I have suffered a terrible injustice?"

Maybe some of the problems in the previous chapters seem trite to someone who has been the victim of tragedy. Can the Bible really help someone who has been raped by their father? Can God's word help someone who has watched their entire family slaughtered before their eyes? What about someone facing death because they have become a Christian? Surely the Bible is not enough in these circumstances?

In Peter's second letter, he reminds us of the importance of Scripture. The Holy Spirit works through Scripture to give us *"everything we need for a godly life"* (2 Pet. 1:3, emphasis added) so that we can be effective and productive in our Christian lives (v. 8). Paul says a similar thing when he writes to Timothy:

All Scripture is God-breathed and is useful for teaching, rebuking, correcting and training in righteousness, so that the servant of God may be thoroughly equipped for every good work (2 Tim. 3:16–17).

Both passages make the claim that Scripture applied to our lives is more than adequate for every situation. A pastor or friend may help us deal with the issues, but that help should focus on helping us learn to use our sword. Apart from that, such mentors should mainly listen, question, love, and pray for and with us. This is so we can think through the issues ourselves.

There are three major and related issues that the victims of injustice need to deal with. The first is related to the injustice that occurred and whether or not God cares. The second is related to anger, hatred and forgiveness, and the third concerns the low self-esteem and false guilt that often plagues victims of such injustice.

Anger is a normal response to injustice. However, if anger isn't dealt with, it soon becomes hatred and bitterness. In the end, these emotions can cause more harm than the original tragedy.

Forgiveness for an injustice or other abuse may seem impossible, but if we don't forgive, we will be the ones who end up suffering the most.

Let's consider each of the three major issues in turn.

1. Why me? Does God care or is He powerless?

Corrie Ten Boom was imprisoned in Ravensbruck concentration camp during World War II because her family had hidden Jews from the Nazis. Apart from her personal suffering, she watched her beloved sister and many others die.[1]

Sokreaksa Himm watched his whole family hacked to death. He was also injured and lay in the grave with their dead bodies before crawling to safety.[2]

I am sure that Satan made each of these people ask, "Why me? Did I do something to deserve this pain or provoke the attack? Is it a punishment from God?" Perhaps they knew they were innocent but wondered if God knew or cared, or was just powerless to help them.

Although these thoughts and questions are natural ones, it is important that we work through them because each can lead us to doubt God's goodness and power. It is very common for people to make assumptions about God's character and then recoil from the horrible god they have conjured up. That is a tragedy, because they run from the only one who can deal with the horrors they have suffered.

It is a long, slow process to take every thought captive and keep them under control and the best way to reflect on the Scriptures necessary is to do it in the company of loving friends, pastors, or counselors, and with much prayer.

* The "Why me?" question is dealt with in several places in Scripture: Job's story; the deaths of eighteen people when a tower collapses (Luke 13); and the healing of the man born blind (John 9; see Chapter 13 for a fuller discussion of these passages). In all these passages, we realize that there is rarely a single reason why things occur. In fact, in Jesus' life we have the final proof that evil can happen to the totally innocent. The law of cause and effect (Karma) is not true. Sometimes we suffer simply because we live in a world in which there is evil and where people choose to rebel against God.

* Does God care? Read passages which speak of God weeping for our pain. Consider Jesus' words in Matthew 23:37 as He looks out over Jerusalem and sees the pain that will come to her.

> Jerusalem, Jerusalem...how often I have longed to gather your children together, as a hen gathers her chicks under her wings.

In John 11, Jesus wept at Lazarus' house. Why does He weep when He knows that He is about to raise Lazarus from the dead? Surely one of the reasons is that He weeps for the pain that His friends have endured and the pain that sickness and death cause to all people.

* Spend time thinking about what it must have meant for Jesus to live in this world. Chapter 13 lists some of the sufferings that Jesus

endured. In addition, Jesus endured the normal pains of sickness, loneliness, grief, and singleness. He must have often felt alone and misunderstood for it wasn't as if there was anyone who was His equal on earth. We cannot accuse Jesus of not understanding our circumstances or being uncaring. Hebrews 4:15 reminds us that Jesus is able to empathize with our weaknesses since He has experienced the same temptations as we have.

* Spend time thinking about God as King and His sovereign control of everything. The stories of Joseph (Gen. 37–50), Daniel (Dan. 1–6) or Jesus can be a huge comfort. They all suffered greatly whilst being innocent of blame. Yet in each of their lives, God worked things out for the good of His Kingdom. What Joseph and Daniel suffered made their character's more like God's and enabled them to have a wide impact so that many others came to follow God too.

* Let's look at Romans 8:28–29 again:

> We know that in all things God works for the good of those who have been called according to his purpose [and this purpose is]...to be conformed to the image of his Son.

We might even die during our suffering (as Corrie Ten Boom's sister did), but these verses promise that if we trust God in our suffering, He will make us more like Jesus. A transformed life will bring others to know Jesus too. In heaven, incredible as it seems, we will rejoice and praise God for what He achieved through our pain.

* Reflect on God as a God of justice. It should bring huge comfort to know that all through Scripture, God sees. His view of the situation is totally unclouded by lack of information or misunderstanding of the issues. God will judge. Wickedness will not escape judgement. Psalm 73 describes a man who struggled with injustice and how he uses his knowledge of God to fight and win the battle of his mind.

Being confident that God will judge and that it is not our role to take revenge (Rom. 12:19), frees us up to face the journey of forgiveness.

2. Forgiveness

Even among Christians, there is some disagreement about what forgiveness involves in practice. For example, whether people should be forgiven if they never repent and how to apply forgiveness in certain situations. However, some things are very clear because the Bible speaks clearly, even shockingly (from our point of view) on this issue.

Some of these passages are listed below.

* Matthew 6:14–15

> For if you forgive other people when they sin against you, your heavenly Father will also forgive you. But if you do not forgive others their sins, your Father will not forgive your sins.

Several times in the Gospels, Jesus makes this point that our being forgiven by God is linked with whether we are willing to forgive others. If we refuse to forgive, then it proves that we don't understand how much God has forgiven us. By refusing to forgive, we refuse to trust that God knows what is best for us. When He tells us to forgive, He is in fact showing us the only way we can be healed. True healing only comes as we let go of anger and bitterness, and choose to forgive.

However, we don't just forgive so we can be forgiven or even for our heart's health, we forgive because to do so brings glory to God. God is also glorified because of the sheer immensity and generosity of His forgiveness. When we choose to forgive others, we proclaim His glory because without the truth of God first forgiving us, we would never have the desire or power to forgive anyone. Every time we choose to forgive someone, it announces the gospel of forgiveness and it is a miracle. When we forgive, people should praise God for enabling this supernatural event to occur.

* Matthew 18:21–35

The parable of the unmerciful servant is one of the clearest passages about forgiveness in the Bible. A servant is forgiven an extremely large debt. He immediately goes out and demands repayment from another servant who owes him a far smaller sum of money. The point of the parable is that God has forgiven us everything and any other person only owes us a small amount in comparison. How then can we withhold forgiveness from anyone?

One possible reason is that we don't understand how sinful we are or how much God has forgiven us. We like to think that we're not so bad. The difference between the wrong that others have done to us and the wrong we have done to God is like the difference in size between a ping-pong ball and the sun!

We need to ask God to reveal more of the extent of our sin. He is a good and gracious God who can be trusted not to overwhelm us with the full story all at once. Regularly thinking of ourselves as the Bible sees us, "as sinners saved by grace," helps us to understand that any sin against us is of a much lesser magnitude than the sin of all the years we lived our lives without God, treating Him as irrelevant.

* Colossians 3:13

> Bear with each other and forgive one another if any of you has a grievance against someone. Forgive as the Lord forgave you.

We are to pass on the forgiveness that God has given us. That means that we are to keep forgiving over and over, "seventy times seven" (that is, we must continue forgiving forever) (Matt. 18:22). Peter's shocked reaction at Jesus' standard reveals how far he still had to go on this issue.

God's forgiveness was costly. It cost Jesus His life and all the griefs of living on this earth. It continues to cost Him immense grief as He identifies with the pain we cause as we continue to sin and suffer the consequences of sin. We must never think that because God lives in heaven, He is removed from our pain. As Isaiah 53 says, He is a "man of suffering and familiar with pain..." Because Jesus lived on earth, He both understands and continues to grieve for our sorrows. He has seen the injustices we suffer and He does care (c.f. Ps. 10:13ff.; Ezek. 6:9).

Because God's forgiveness of our sins is costly, we should not be surprised that our forgiveness of others also has a cost. As a friend noted in a sermon, there are three costs to us, as we need to promise:[3]

i. Not to bring up the act and use it against the perpetrator.

You might feel that you have a right to bring it up again, after all you were hurt, but in forgiveness, you forgo that right, and choose not to bring it up.

ii. Not to make other people aware of it.

iii. Not to keep dwelling on it yourself.

God's forgiveness is ongoing and so ours needs to be the same. Hebrews 8:12 quotes Jeremiah 31:34, which says,

> I [God] will forgive their wickedness, and will remember their sins no more.

It is not that God has a poor memory but rather that He chooses to act as though there was no previous sin.

When I was a teenager, an adult became very angry at me over a minor misunderstanding. I became fearful of them because I no longer knew when they might lose their temper at me. I quickly realized that whether or not I was in the wrong initially, I was wrong in refusing to forgive them. I chose to forgive them, even though they did not say sorry to me (they probably didn't even notice the incident or realize how it was damaging our relationship). Perhaps it would have been more sensible if I had confronted them over it. Instead, I worked through my own attitudes before God and repented as I needed to. Then I chose to apply the forgiveness that I had received from Jesus to forgive this person. However, the memory of the deed would often come to my mind and even as I write, I can remember the horrible feeling. But forgiveness means that I must keep choosing to forgive them each time the memories resurface. Forgiveness is very much a continual process, an ongoing application of the blood of Jesus, to a situation and our memories of it.

As time has passed, I find the sting has lessened and it is easier to deal with the memories. I have chosen to relate to the person who hurt me as though they never hurt me. Amazingly, I now have a close friendship with this person and their family. I shudder to think what I would have missed out on if I had refused to forgive. The cost for not forgiving is great too.

What will this forgiveness look like? Does my forgiving someone mean that I am saying that what they have done is okay, that I condone their sin? The cross of Christ tells us clearly that sin does matter. God doesn't just smile, pat us on the head and say, "It doesn't matter, just don't do it again."

A god who did that would be a monster because he would be saying that incest, murder, jealousy, divorce and all pain and injustice were no big deal. Who would want to serve such a god? The cross shows us once that sin does matter; it cannot be dealt with easily. In fact, the *only* way that our mortal sin disease can be dealt with is if a perfect god takes our sin upon himself and suffers in our place. Sin mattered so much that it cost the precious blood of Jesus to deal with its horrendous results and so when we forgive, we are not saying sin does not matter. If we love someone, we will never say that what they did does not matter. Instead, we will show it does matter by explaining the gospel as the only way that sin can be dealt with. We will then explain that we can only forgive because we have Jesus' power in us: the power He used to forgive us. Such words are powerful and liberating, for they are saying, "I'm not going to treat you based on how you treated me but on how God has treated me in Jesus."

Do I only forgive someone if they are sorry for what they did?

Interestingly, most of the commands to forgive others come with no preconditions. We forgive because Christ forgave us and because it is essential for our spiritual (and emotional and physical) health that we do so. We forgive out of obedience to Jesus, not because we feel like it. I imagine that for some situations, it is going to be a constant choice to remind ourselves of God's forgiveness to us and then choosing to forgive, again and again. Satan will try and remind us of the other person's sin, but we must counter with God's word.

However, Luke 17:3 does contain a precondition.[4] It says, "If your brother or sister sins against you, rebuke them; and if they repent, forgive them." Does this mean that if someone refuses to repent, that we are freed from our need to forgive? If so, that would go against all the other passages of Scripture on the issue.

It is perhaps helpful to see forgiveness as having two components, a vertical and a horizontal component. The vertical part of forgiveness is the relationship between us and God. Our sin requires that we first repent in order for the forgiveness to be applied to that sin. It is not that we earn forgiveness by our repentance but simply that that is how it works. Forgiveness is available because of Jesus' death on the cross but it is useless to us unless we ask for it. We must first acknowledge our sin, repent and ask for God's forgiveness.

The horizontal part of forgiveness is person to person. Once we have been forgiven by God, then we must demonstrate our understanding of that forgiveness by forgiving others, regardless of whether or not they repent. This kind of forgiveness demands a change of attitude on our part. On the cross, Jesus asked for forgiveness for those killing him and Stephen asked God to forgive those stoning him, even though there was no immediate desire to repent from the perpetrators. Such a response is essential for our relationship with God to be right.

However, for our earthly relationships to be restored (i.e. for reconciliation to happen), it seems that the offender must repent. It is not until they come to an awareness of the gravity of their sin, and repent before God and then to us, that the relationship can be fully restored. In his book, *Unpacking Forgiveness*,[5] Brauns writes that

> God's forgiveness is gracious, but not free…it is conditional…It is a commitment…it lays the groundwork for and begins the process of

reconciliation, [but that it] does not mean the elimination of all consequences.

He defines God's forgiveness as:

> A commitment by the one true God to pardon graciously those who repent and believe so that they are reconciled to him, although this commitment does not eliminate all consequences.[6]

This is demonstrated in the case of David's sin. His repentance does not eliminate the consequences of his action. Uriah was still dead, Bathsheba was still pregnant and her child died as the consequence. David still had to live with his regrets and yet he could still have a restored relationship with God because of God's graciousness to him (2 Sam. 11–12).

One of the consequences that may not be eliminated is a justifiable lack of trust and a wariness of placing yourself in danger again. This is particularly true in cases of sexual abuse. It would be extremely foolish, once having forgiven someone, to then place yourself trustingly in private with that person again. Indeed it would be wise to say that you should never again be alone with that person and if it is necessary to meet with them, you should ensure that there is always someone else present.

Another step in the forgiveness process is to recognize that justice is God's business. He sees all and He will act.

* Romans 12:17–21

> Do not repay anyone evil for evil...If it is possible, as far as it depends on you, live at peace with everyone. Do not take revenge...but leave room for God's wrath, for it is written: "It is mine to avenge; I will repay," says the Lord. On the contrary: "If your enemy is hungry, feed him...In doing this, you will heap burning coals on his head." Do not be overcome by evil, but overcome evil with good.

We must recognize that we have neither the power nor wisdom to punish appropriately and trust that God, who sees everything, will judge justly in His own time. We often desire revenge but God desires that everyone should come to know and honor Him. Our forgiveness and not taking revenge may be the exact thing that wins our tormentor to the Lord and so transforms them.

Does this mean that Christians will never take anyone to court or pursue criminal proceedings? Not at all, but it would be important for us to check our motivations for why we're doing it. If our desire is not revenge, but to stop further injustice or harm happening, then court proceedings might be essential.

3. Forgiveness and trauma

Another attack that Satan makes on victims is to convince them that their suffering was somehow partly their fault. It is then so easy to have false guilt along the lines of, "If I hadn't driven the car that day, then maybe my son would still be alive."

Guilt (false or otherwise) can be dealt with by following the steps described in Chapter 10. Repenting as necessary and then trusting that any sin has been dealt with. With false guilt, we need to apply truth to the situation. For example, the victim of incest needs to remind themselves that the sin is not theirs. A person does not need to feel guilty or be ashamed of what another has done to them.

Sadly, low self-esteem and self-hate are common in those who have been raped or abused. (Refer to Chapter 12 for verses to deal with low self-esteem). This kind of abuse affects whole families. A loving friend who listens and points them constantly to Jesus and His word is invaluable. The focus should be on meditating on what God thinks of us.

Sokreaksa Himm was a teenager when the Khmer Rouge came to power in Cambodia. After much suffering, which included near starvation, many threats of death and having a brother almost beaten to death, his family was herded into the jungle in 1977. They were forced to dig a large pit. The whole family, including parents, nine siblings, a nephew and a sister-in-law, were hacked to death with picks and shovels and fell into the hole. Sokreaksa fell into the grave, injured but alive and covered by the dead bodies of his parents and siblings. He was the only one to survive and later managed to dig his way out. He then spent months in grief and near starvation in the jungle before being taken in by a brave neighbor.

Later, he escaped through the minefields to Thailand and was eventually allowed to migrate to Canada. Along the way he became a Christian and God began the long process of healing his severe post-traumatic stress disorder. He often had panic attacks and severe recurring nightmares where he re-lived his traumas. Eventually healing progressed and he wanted to return to Cambodia to serve the Lord there, being convinced that his country needed to know the power of God's forgiveness.[7]

While in Cambodia he was convicted that God wanted him to meet up with and forgive the killers of his family. For a long time, the killers refused to meet him, believing that he was masking his desire for revenge with strange talk about forgiveness. However, he was eventually able to meet with them and share God's forgiveness with them.

In the second volume of his autobiography, Sokreaksa Himm wrote,

> Twelve years after forgiving my family's killers I observe that my life has changed dramatically. I am healthier than I was and the depression has left me. I no longer need tranquilizers because the Prince of Peace rules my life. My mind is at peace and the joy of life has been restored. The prison door of my heart has been broken open, hatred has been uprooted and bitterness has been washed away by the water of life from the Holy Spirit...The fire of anger has subsided and I am at peace. I have found that it is impossible to remove the anger at what the killers did, but I have learned to over-

come its power. It no longer affects my life, nor can it make my life miserable.[8]

Reflection Questions:

1. In what areas have you found it hard to forgive?

2. Do you agree or disagree with the views expressed in this chapter? It's okay to disagree as long as your view can stand up to the standards of Scripture. Go and search God's word for His answers.

3. Create a list of principles, verses and stories to help with your specific situation.

Prayer Suggestions:

1. Spend time reflecting on God's forgiveness. Apply this particularly to yourself and praise God.

2. Ask God to reveal to you anyone that you have not forgiven. Ask for forgiveness for your bitterness, hardness of heart or whatever is appropriate for your situation.

3. Ask for strength to forgive and keep forgiving.

---

1. Corrie Ten Boom, John Sherrill, and Elizabeth Sherrill, *The Hiding Place* (London: Hodder and Stoughton, 2004).
2. Sokreaksa Himm, *The Tears of My Soul* (Oxford: Monarch Books, 2006).
3. Kevin Reid's sermon headings.
4. I am indebted to a Bible college friend, Kevin Reid, for pointing out this verse to me and for allowing me to read a sermon he preached on forgiveness. I have used many of his points and ideas in this chapter.
5. Chris Brauns, *Unpacking Forgiveness* (Wheaton: Crossway Books, 2008), 45–49.
6. Brauns, *Unpacking Forgiveness*, 51.
7. Sokreaksa Himm, *The Tears of My Soul* (Oxford: Monarch Books, 2006).
8. Sokreaksa Himm, *After the Heavy Rain* (Oxford: Monarch Books, 2007), 123.

CONCLUSION

This book has focused on learning how to use the sword of the Spirit, which is God's word, to win the battle for our minds. Like most battles of this nature, it is not a once and for all time event. Applying God's word is not a magical abracadabra formula that solves all our problems in a millisecond. Rather, like sword fighting, it takes time to get into practice and to learn to fight effectively and efficiently. Initially, our sword fighting muscles will ache and we will get bruised and fall over because we haven't yet mastered the skills we need. Just as in any battle, we will use a lot of energy as we fight to take every thought captive, but over time and with much practice, sword fighting will become automatic.

I find it much easier to practice when I am physically, emotionally, and spiritually fit. Conversely, when I am not fit in all these areas, I will be much more vulnerable to Satan's attacks. He never plays fair, so we need to persevere in the strength of the Spirit we have been given.

My prayer is that applying the principles in this book will lead you to believe and store these things deep in your heart instead of just knowing about them on the surface of your mind. May they become part of who you are and may you then be able to pass on what you have learned to bless those you disciple.

Below is one final story. An excellent example of sword fighting in an almost impossible to forgive situation.

Corrie Ten Boom's family were watchmakers in the town of Haarlem in the Netherlands. During World War 2, they sheltered Jewish people in a secret room in their home. Her excellent book, *The Hiding Place*, goes into great detail about this time.[1]

Eventually, the family was betrayed and Corrie's father died in prison. Corrie and her sister, Betsie, ended up in Ravensbruck concentration camp in Germany where Betsie also died.

After the war, Corrie had a ministry of reconciliation around Europe. Listen to a part of her story in her own words.[2] Please note how Corrie reminds herself of Scriptures and how little time she has to win the battle.

> It was 1947 and I had come from Holland to defeated Germany with the message that God forgives.
>
> It was the truth they needed most to hear in that bitter, bombed-out land, and I gave them my favourite mental picture…"When we confess our sins," I said, "God casts them into the deepest ocean…I believe God then places a sign out there that says, NO FISHING ALLOWED."
>
> …And that's when I saw him, working his way forward… One moment I saw the overcoat and brown hat; the next, a blue uniform and a visored cap with its skull and crossbones. It came back with a rush: the huge room with its harsh overhead lights; the pathetic pile of dresses and shoes in the center of the floor; the shame of walking naked past this man. I could see my sister's frail form ahead of me, ribs sharp beneath the parchment skin…
>
> The place was Ravensbruck and the man who was making his way forward had been a guard—one of the most cruel guards.

Now he was in front of me, hand thrust out: "A fine message, Fraulein! How good it is to know that...all our sins are at the bottom of the sea!"

And I, who had spoken so glibly of forgiveness, fumbled in my pocketbook rather than take that hand. He would not remember me, of course—how could he remember one prisoner among those thousands of women?

But I remembered him and the leather crop swinging from his belt. I was face-to-face with one of my captors and my blood seemed to freeze.

"You mentioned Ravensbruck in your talk," he was saying. "I was a guard there." No, he did not remember me.

"But since that time," he went on, "I have become a Christian. I know that God has forgiven me for the cruel things I did there, but I would like to hear it from your lips as well. Fraulein,"—again the hand came out—"will you forgive me?"

And I stood there—I whose sins had again and again to be forgiven–and could not forgive. Betsie had died in that place—could he erase her slow terrible death simply for the asking?

It could not have been many seconds that he stood there —hand held out—but to me it seemed hours as I wrestled with the most difficult thing that I had ever had to do.

For I had to do it—I knew that. The message that God forgives has a prior condition: that we forgive those who have injured us. "If you do not forgive men their trespasses," Jesus says, "neither will your father in heaven forgive your trespasses."

I knew it not only as a commandment of God, but as a daily experience. Since the end of the war I had had a home in Holland for victims of Nazi brutality. Those who were able to forgive their former enemies were able also to return to the outside world and rebuild their lives, no matter what the physical scars. Those who nursed their bitterness remained invalids. It was as simple and as horrible as that.

And still I stood there with the coldness clutching my heart. But forgiveness is not an emotion—I knew that too. Forgiveness is an act of the will, and the will can function regardless of the temperature of the heart. "Jesus help me!" I prayed silently. "I can lift my hand. I can do that much. You supply the feeling."

And so woodenly, mechanically, I thrust my hand into the one stretched out to me. And as I did, an incredible thing took place. The current started in my shoulder, raced down my arm, sprang into our joined hands. And then this healing warmth seemed to flood my whole being, bringing tears to my eyes.

"I forgive you brother!" I cried. "With all my heart."

For a long moment we grasped each other's hands, the former guard and the former prisoner. I had never known God's love so intensely as I did then. But even so, I realized it was not my love. I had tried, and did not have the power. It was the power of the Holy Spirit.

May the Holy Spirit grant you the power to wield your sword to defeat the enemy's plans.

---

1. Corrie Ten Boom, John Sherrill, and Elizabeth Sherrill, *The Hiding Place* (London: Hodder and Stoughton, 2004).
2. Corrie Ten Boom and Jamie Buckingham, *Tramp for the Lord* (London: Hodder and Stoughton, 1974), 55-57.

FOUND THIS BOOK HELPFUL?

Reviews sell books.

As this book is independently published, the only way it will be discovered by readers is if you get excited about it. Online reviews are one way to share your enthusiasm.

A book can never have too many reviews.

How to write a review – easy as 1-2-3

1. Write a few sentences about why you liked the book. Maybe one sentence about what kinds of people might like this book. Even one word turns a mere star rating into a review.
2. Upload a review - the same review can be copied and pasted to each site. The priority sites are book selling sites + Goodreads, BookBub, Koorong (for Australians) ...
3. If you loved the book please also share your review on your personal social media. Anywhere you can spread the word is appreciated.

STORYTELLER FRIENDS

Becoming a **storyteller friend** (https://subscribe.storytellerchristine.com/) will ensure you don't miss out on new books, deals and behind the scenes book news. Once you're signed up, check your junk mail or the promotions folder (gmail addresses) for the confirmation email. This two-stage process ensures only true storyteller friends can join.

Facebook: As well as a public author page, I also have a VIP group (https://www.facebook.com/groups/242910632748639) which you need to ask permission to join. This group is where updates and prayer requests for my writing ministry are shared. The group also has the fun of voting for titles and covers...

Website https://storytellerchristine.com/

Pinterest – many resources related to Bible storytelling and my books.

BookBub - allows you to see my top book recommendations and be alerted to any new releases and special deals. It is free to join. https://www.bookbub.com/profile/christine-dillon

NON-FICTION BY CHRISTINE DILLON

1-2-1 Discipleship: Helping One Another Grow Spiritually (Ross-shire: Christian Focus, 2009).

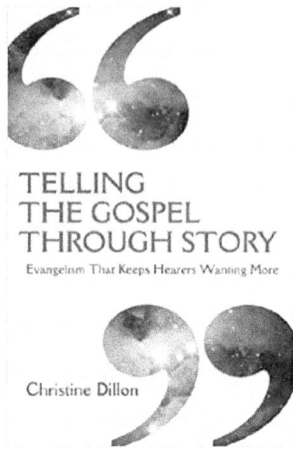

Telling the Gospel Through Story: Evangelism That Keeps Hearers Wanting More (Downer's Grove: IVP, 2012).

Stories Aren't Just For Kids: Busting 10 Myths About Bible Storytelling (2017).

This book is free for subscribers. It's a taster book and includes many testimonies to get you excited about the potential of Bible storying. All these books have also been translated into Chinese.

The Sword Fighting book has just been translated into German.

FICTION BY CHRISTINE DILLON

The novels are widely available in print, LARGE PRINT, ebook, and audio. They can be bought directly from the author (https://payhip.com/ChristineDillon) or via many online sellers.

Grace in Strange Disguise - Book 1
Grace in the Shadows - Book 2
Grace in Deep Waters - Book 3
Grace in the Desert - Book 4
Grace Beneath the Frost - Book 5
Grace Across the Miles - Book 6

AUTHOR'S NOTE

This book has had a complicated journey to publication. It was one of the earliest books I wrote but it has been sitting unpublished for twelve years.

In 2008, I was invited to dinner and one of the men there heard me talking about some of the sword fighting ideas. He begged me to write a book. He insistence drove me to write the book immediately, and I sent off the draft to him for his comments.

The resultant critique was so harsh that I didn't look at the manuscript for another year. If I hadn't just signed a contract for *1-2-1 Discipleship*, it may have totally derailed my entire writing journey. I certainly lost the little confidence I had.

One year later, I told a pastoral friend about the critique I'd received. He offered to read the manuscript and he gave some helpful comments.

This really underlined for me the difference between critiques that are strong, but kindly worded, and those that are not.

I rewrote the manuscript but for the next twelve years it was only read by people who asked me about the subject.

In 2019, as I wrote the first draft of my fourth novel it became clear that the issue of sword fighting would be part of the plot. I could not say much in the fiction format but I wondered if the time had come to publish the non-fiction book.

I started some edits but soon became discouraged. At that point, two friends, quite independently from each other called me and asked me if I would publish that "useful manuscript." I took that as God's prompting and started rewriting in earnest. Then with much trepidation I sent it to a group of beta readers including quite a few working in paid Christian ministry. The feedback was very clear; publish this, we need this book.

My prayer is that this book will impact the daily lives of many Christians. Christians who have struggled with one or other of these issues that are dragging them down.

ACKNOWLEDGMENTS

No book is a solitary effort. My team is terrific and this time included some new people, since non-fiction is very different to fiction. Several of you I've never met.

Thank you first to Jesus who used Kevin to encourage me about the content so that I didn't destroy this manuscript.

Thank you to the few people who applied the content into their lives over the past twelve years and in doing so reminded me of the manuscript's existence.

Charissa M., and Cathy S., thank you for urging me to publish this and to my beta readers: Rhonda B., Alastair C., Judy D., and Ngaira S. Your comments were helpful and encouraged me to keep going.

Thank you to the eagle-eyed proofreaders: Kate B., Sashi G., Anne M., Jane P., Lizzie R., and Kim W. It has been even more difficult this time as you had to proofread according to U.S. guidelines, not Australian. It's not easy to deal with different spellings and punctuation rules.

This is the first time since 2011 that I've had a non-fiction book professionally edited. Thank you Nola Passmore.

Once again Joy Lankshear has designed an amazing cover. I particularly appreciate that she is willing for people in my VIP Facebook group to comment on a range of designs and then adjusts her design according to their feedback.

ABOUT THE AUTHOR

Christine has worked with OMF International since 1999, mostly in Taiwan and recently within Australia.

It's best not to ask Christine, "Where are you from?" She's a missionary kid who isn't sure if she should say her passport country (Australia) or her Dad's country (New Zealand) or where she's spent most of her life (Taiwan, Malaysia and the Philippines).

Christine used to be a physiotherapist, but now writes "storyteller" on airport forms. She spends most of her time either telling Bible stories or training others to do so.

In her spare time, Christine loves all things active – hiking, cycling, swimming, snorkelling. But she also likes reading and genealogical research.

Connect with Christine
www.storytellerchristine.com/

facebook.com/storytellerchristine
bookbub.com/profile/christine-dillon
pinterest.com/storytellerchristine